UNLOCKING YOUR POTENTIAL

£9.99

D1102909

Some other titles in this series

Achieving Personal Well-Being	Managing Your Time
Awakening the Writer Within	Managing Yourself
Building Self-Esteem	Mastering Public Speaking
Conducting Effective Negotiations	Maximising Your Memory
Controlling Anxiety	Passing Exams without Anxiety
Critical Thinking for Students	Passing that Interview
Getting That Job	Self-Counselling
Healing the Hurt Within	Staying Ahead at Work
How to Market Yourself	Studying at University
How to Study and Learn	Studying for a Degree
Making Decisions	Thriving on Stress
Managing Successful Teams	Winning Presentations

Other titles in preparation

The How To Series now contains more than 200 titles in the following categories:

Business & Management	Personal Finance
Computer Basics	Self-Development
General Reference	Small Business
Jobs & Careers	Student Handbooks
Living & Working Abroad	Successful Writing

Please send for a free copy of the latest catalogue for full details (see back cover for address).

SELF-DEVELOPMENT

UNLOCKING YOUR POTENTIAL

How to master your mind,
life and destiny

Dr Peter Marshall, BA, BSc Econ, PhD

How To Books

NORTHBROOK   COLLEGE
DESIGN + TECHNOLOGY

616066	Class No 158.1
MACAULAY	24 Aug 1999
Location.	WE		

Cartoons by Mike Flanagan

British Library Cataloguing in Publication Data
A catalogue record for this book is available from the British Library.

© Copyright 1998 by Peter Marshall.

First published by How To Books Ltd, 3 Newtec Place,
Magdalen Road, Oxford OX4 1RE. United Kingdom.
Tel: (01865) 793806. Fax: (01865) 248780.

All rights reserved. No part of this work may be reproduced or stored in an
information retrieval system (other than for purposes of review) without the
express permission of the Publisher in writing.

Note: The material contained in this book is set out in good faith for
general guidance and no liability can be accepted for loss or expense
incurred as a result of relying in particular circumstances on statements
made in the book. The laws and regulations are complex and liable to
change, and readers should check the current position with the relevant
authorities before making personal arrangements.

Produced for How To Books by Deer Park Productions.
Typeset by PDQ Typesetting, Stoke-on-Trent, Staffs.
Printed and bound by Cromwell Press, Trowbridge, Wiltshire.

Contents

Preface

The Romans used to say: *Video meliora proboque deteriora sequo.* It means 'I can see what I ought and ought not to do and I go and do the latter.' How many times has this been true for you? Nor is it only our actions which are often self-destructive, but our feelings and beliefs about ourselves too. As I pointed out in *How to Study and Learn* (in this series), little if anything limits people's achievement more than their own self-doubts and these are often unfounded. We may, in fact, be well aware that we ought to think more highly of ourselves than we do. Why do people defeat themselves in this way?

It's all down to memory again. In *Maximising Your Memory* (also in this series) I showed how our memory abilities can be used to our best advantage. This books deals with how they sometimes work against us. If you really want to be the master of your mind, life and destiny you need to understand how this happens and how you can liberate yourself from these effects.

This book will show you how to do it. It will introduce you to objective techniques for overcoming the limiting effects of the past, including: repressed conflicts, the effects of conditioning, inappropriate conceptualisations, limiting states of mind, negative thinking and the expectations of others. It is aimed at all who want to change their lives for the better and who have the courage to breach the walls which hold them back.

Peter Marshall

LIBRARY
NORTHBROOK COLLEGE
BROADWATER ROAD
WORTHING
WEST SUSSEX
BN14 8HJ
TEL: 01903 606451

1
Overhauling Your Conditioning

UNDERSTANDING WHY PEOPLE KEEP MAKING THE SAME MISTAKES

Why do some people always seem to be trying, but never quite making it? Why do some people seem to have more crises than others? Why do some people always end up in bad relationships with violent or unreliable partners? Why do some people seem to have more accidents than most? Why do some seem to have all the bad luck and little or none of the good?

In the most conspicuous cases it is not due to lack of intelligence, skill, will-power or resources. If they had little intelligence, skill and will they would be unlikely to try in the first place. No, the reasons are much more subtle than this.

As people develop, they begin to aim for certain things in life and learn how to go about achieving them. Rarely, though, do they learn to control the subtle forces which undermine their efforts.

Here are some typical examples of how people shoot themselves in the foot.

Escaping from one bad relationship into another
The problem may be:

- unreliability
- unfaithfulness
- violence
- relationship unsatisfactory in other ways.

Some people respond by breaking the relationship, but returning to the same partner again and again. Others tend to find a new relationship with the potential for the same problems as before.

Kicking yourself for missing glaring opportunities

How often have you seen a glaring opportunity but avoided it, thinking, 'If it's that certain why haven't others taken it up?' Then it has 'come up trumps' and you have sworn you will not let the chance slip by again – but you have. This applies to various aspects of life, for example:

- business and financial
- social
- personal relationships.

Playing the born loser

Some people's favourite saying seems to be 'Why does it always happen to me?' They seem to be dogged with simple bad luck. Again, it can apply to various aspects of life:

- business and financial matters
- social
- personal relationships.

Underachieving

People underachieve in various ways and it spoils their quality of life. By underachievement, I mean achieving *less than they wish to and are capable of,* not *less than others wish them to.* This can occur:

- in their career
- in their education.

People may underachieve in relation to:

- the achievement levels of their peers
- their achievement in other subjects
- their general ability
- other periods of their lives.

The most able individuals are prone to underachievement, because of put downs by others – teachers, parents, peers, etc. They sometimes fool about to hide their high ability and avoid the unpleasantness of these.

We are our memories

The causes of self-defeating behaviour are rooted in memory. My other book – *Maximising Your Memory* – deals with the positive aspects of memory; this book is aimed at revealing the negative aspects and teaching how to overcome the effects of inappropriate storage.

We store every aspect of experience

Our minds store every aspect of experience – event, understanding and feelings. Physiological evidence confirms this. These understandings and feelings will be evoked when comparable events occur and they will guide our responses. Conversely, our desire to relive the stored feelings will influence the way we behave. The next section provides a brief résumé of how our store of experiential data accumulates and how it influences all future behaviour. It also deals with how the process sometimes seems to backfire.

Human beings have instinctual wants. If that was all there was to us, though, we would just reach out and grab everything we wanted, taking it from anyone. Only the strongest would survive. We are more complicated than that. It is this very complexity that can undermine many otherwise high calibre people's success in life.

Feelings

The moment we are born we are launched into entirely different conditions from those we had, hitherto, always known. The first feeling we experience in the world is discomfort, for new situations are always uncomfortable.

We relate all experiences to previous situations stored in our minds. These are known as **schemata** (plural of schema). That's how we make sense of them. So each new event jogs our memory to recall a previous similar event. With the recall we actually relive the feeling we felt then, for it was attached to it when it was stored.

The first feelings we store

The first time we experience any kind of separation after our birth we relate it to the experience of birth itself. That is the only stored experience up to that time which is in any way comparable, the only experience of separation. Thus, we relive the feeling, to some extent, and discomfort is felt.

Subsequent feelings

Within minutes of being born babies are washed and reunited with their mothers. This negates the separation to some degree and reduces the discomfort. We become aware, therefore, at some level, that a source of comfort is available.

Soon we begin to realise, however, that the source of comfort can be removed as quickly as it was given. We become aware, too, that it tends to be removed at those times when we try to satisfy our instinctual urges. This creates **anxiety**. We also come to know the cross looks and the harsh sounds that signal rejection – the threat of separation again.

Life becomes a perpetual striving for approval from our parents and others whose approval matters to us – teachers, employers, husband or wife, for example. This becomes the motive force that will shape our lives. We will always be at least slightly insecure (this is the norm) and we will orientate our efforts towards avoiding insecurity.

A full store of emotional feelings

As we struggle to manage the competing demands of our nature and our need for approval, our store of emotional experiences grows. By the time we are five years of age we have experienced just about every variation of emotional feeling there is. Each one is stored with the circumstances from which it derived. For the rest of our lives we will seek to gain the positive feelings and avoid the negative ones which we have learned, in our earliest years, derive from particular behaviours.

Understandings

Besides the stored feelings, which are known as **child data**, we also store understandings.

Uncritical acceptance

Many of the understandings we take on board in our childhood are accepted uncritically. Their source is what our parents and other authority figures (teachers, etc) say to us and to others. It is, thus, known as **parent data**. We infer what they think from what they say. Without adequate means of challenging it we assume that it is the right way to think. This is especially the case in the first five years of life.

Examples of parent data

This kind of data includes the moral do's and don'ts:

- What is right and what is wrong.

- What we should and should not do.
- What we should think and aspire to.

It often comes in commands such as:

- Speak only when you are spoken to.
- Don't boast.
- Don't expect too much and you won't be disappointed.
- Don't get ideas above your station.
- Never forget your roots.
- Don't get too big for your boots.
- Don't show off.
- Get a proper job.
- Don't be pushy.
- They'll laugh at you, if you apply.
- People like us don't go to university.
- Stick with what you've got, don't go chasing fortunes.
- Know your station in life.

This kind of data also includes:

- judgements of individuals and types of people
- establishment of limits
- opinions on discipline
- guidance – how to do this or that
- maintenance of tradition.

When this kind of information is delivered in a stern voice it will be difficult to override.

Approval and encouragement

Parent data also includes approval and encouragement. Some children receive less of this than others and some receive virtually none at all. The two ends of the spectrum of this type of data tend to be referred to as **the nurturing parent**, and **the critical parent**.

As we grow, we progressively develop minds of our own. We employ rational thought, the rules of logic and belief in what we see with our own eyes. This is known as **adult data**, or the adult part of the psyche.

It is different from the child in us, which responds to feelings, and the parent part of us, which works from nagging echoes of wisdom we long ago took for granted. The adult in us is the mature part of the psyche which equips us to take on the world by ourselves.

By the time we are adults in the physiological sense, if things have gone as they should, the adult part of our psyche will be firmly in the driving seat of our minds. The effects of the child and parent will still be felt, though. These parts of our psyche will still have their expression from time to time. Indeed, life would be drab if they didn't.

The child is given expression when we are having fun, for example. It provides our sense of excitement, our desire for achievement and the range of emotional experiences that give life its flavour.

The parent in us acts as the keeper of our conscience and without this we would not be social beings.

In the ideal outcome, though, the adult part of the psyche has the upper hand and can control the other parts where necessary. Furthermore, it knows best how to satisfy the demands of the child part, the part that strives, desires, needs and feels, the part which gives us our motivation for life.

This is made easier by the fact that only one of these parts of the psyche can be dominant at any one time. The other parts can nag at it and influence its freedom of action, but unless the adult part allows them to replace it, they will only have a subordinate role. Unfortunately, that subordinate influence can sometimes be quite persuasive and it is to such situations that this chapter now turns.

When things go wrong

Things sometimes go a little wrong in the process of development. Sometimes parents are rather unresponsive and children have to work hard to gain attention. The ways they manage to attract it are stored, along with the feelings of attention themselves. This kind of child data is known as the **adapted child**.

Over-compliance

Habitual over-compliance is one kind of adapted child response. Perpetual, extreme agreement, for the sake of being seen to be good is the seed of an adult, habitual *yes person*. Such people appear to have no mind of their own. If you've ever watched BBC's popular comedy series *The Brittas Empire*, the character of Colin is a classic example. It is this kind of behaviour that is primarily associated with approval in his mind, so it is repeated often.

Nobody respects a habitual yes person, though. Their affirmations only represent compliance, not true agreement, so they will never be taken seriously, or trusted with responsibility.

Stored negative attention

Another kind of adapted child response is negative attention-seeking. When a child finds it cannot gain positive attention it will seek the negative kind. Being punished is better than being ignored. Laziness, deviousness, bullying, arrogance, habitual lateness, untidiness, failure and noncompliance for its own sake are all examples of such adapted child responses.

These become stored with the experience of gaining attention. They will be repeated habitually in adulthood, because of their attention-gaining potential.

Conflicting parent responses

Sometimes parents, or other authority figures, give conflicting signals, at times rewarding and at others admonishing. Sometimes they even appear totally unmoved when a child does something which deserves a show of approval.

Discordant or ambiguous parent responses tend to be blocked before they are recorded. The child grows up not being sure how to gain approval, how to escape the discomfort. They emerge neurotic, and neurotic behaviour is often self-defeating and energy-sapping.

Lack of approval

Where parents are over harsh and never rewarding, the child learns it can never get any comfort from them, however hard it tries. It might as well give up trying and just get on with feeding its instinctual wants. The child grows up anti-social.

Nobody's upbringing is perfect. Some emerge with few problems and many advantages. Life appears to be more or less a continuous run of green lights for them. Others emerge with just about every drawback that could be envisaged. Most lie somewhere between these two extremes.

If something is holding you back and it's not a lack of intelligence, skill or determination, the fault is likely to be somewhere in your conditioning for life. This conditioning is your accumulated store of events, understandings and feelings. This book aims to help you uncover and overcome the problem.

Recognising some effects of inappropriate conditioning

Affairs of the heart
Some people avoid approaching members of opposite sex, for fear of rejection.

Social
Some people avoid new social situations. Others are afraid to affiliate with their ideal social group, because they feel they would appear inferior, or would let themselves down.

Educational/professional
Some people may wish to apply for a better job, or get themselves a better education, but doubt their capability. They may even feel people would laugh at their ambitions.

Here are some of the ways such maladjustment may present itself.

How stored experiences can restrict us

- feelings of inferiority
- unjustified self-doubts
- reticence
- shyness
- withdrawal
- inaction
- over-cautiousness
- fear of failure
- the once bitten twice shy excuse
- avoidance of situations that could be positive, e.g. meeting people
- fear of rejection
- fear of being isolated
- fear of not being able to cope
- fear of put downs

- avoidance of unfamiliar situations – including success!

How stored memories can make us fail
Stored, unfavourable responses can cause people to defeat themselves in the following ways:

- setting impossible goals
- selecting impossible partner choices
- playing the born loser
- allowing themselves to be victims of matrimonial violence
- being accident prone.

The undesirable legacies
The legacies of unfavourable aspects of our development, which lie at the root of self-defeating behaviour, come in the following forms:

- internal dialogue
- exclusion
- contamination.

Internal dialogue
When you have the intelligence, education, skill and will-power, but you still don't seem to be able to cope with things well, internal dialogues might be sapping your energy. Some people are frequently preoccupied with torturing themselves about what they have failed to do, yet mentally defending their actions with excuses. Do you do this?

It is known as internal dialogue, because two parts of the psyche are communicating with each other. These are the child part (which feels ashamed of failure) and the parent part (which condemns the child part). The parent is admonishing, while the child is seeking to excuse itself.

The dialogue goes on and on and gets nowhere, but it takes energy to keep it going. If you use your mental energy for this you do not have it available for meaningful and useful work.

An example of an internal dialogue between the *critical parent* and *child* parts of a person's psyche might be:

Internalised parent: If only I'd been quicker off the mark, I'd have beaten Armstrong's to the post and got the order.

Internalised child:	But how was I to know they were also tendering?
Internalised parent:	It was obvious they would be tendering.
Internalised child:	I had other demands upon my time.

Exclusion of part of the psyche
Do you spend most of your time helping, or criticising, others while your own interests suffer through lack of attention? Are you, for example:

- the *do-gooder* who never has time for their own advancement?

- the *matchmaker* who returns to their lonely home each night?

- the perpetual *yes person* who just attracts contempt and wonders why they command no respect?

- the compulsive *gambler* who follows winning streaks and relies on a belief that runs of bad luck must change?

If so, you may be excluding a part of your psyche (child, adult or parent). In so doing you are depriving yourself of the benefit that part plays in keeping your performance balanced.

Exclusions are not always as simple as this. Some people exclude only a facet of a psyche element, e.g. the natural child, or the critical parent. Alternatively, they may exclude more than one part, or facet, e.g. exclusion of the adult and natural child.

Contamination
Although only one of the three parts of the psyche can be dominant at any one time, other parts can interfere with its function to some degree. We call this contamination. The child or the parent can, for example, impinge upon the functioning of the adult. This will make it less rational, reasonable, or open-minded than it ought to be. When unfounded child or parent data is accepted as true, the adult part of the psyche rationalises and justifies it in whatever way it can.

Feelings of inferiority, fear of not being liked, fear of rejection and unjustified self-doubts are some examples of feelings that can prevent the most able of people from fulfilling their potential. These are typical child feelings that may impinge upon the functioning of the adult part of the psyche.

Another example of the problem is when unrealistic perceptions and imaginative ideas cloud an otherwise sound and rational judgement. The compulsive gambler who believes he is on a winning streak is an example. Another is the business executive who will not make a deal on Friday 13th.

Where the adult is contaminated with parent data the individual's social interactions may be marked by a hypercritical and interfering nature, or being caring to the point of self-sacrifice.

Where attention seeking data is negative
Yet another example of how stored data can handicap people is where an individual received a predominance of negative attention as a child – admonishment, punishment, condemnation, etc (see page 15). Such an individual may, without realising, seek negative responses as an adult, because that has become the kind of attention they have best learned how to attain and handle.

If a child received a predominance of negative attention as a child it will seek negative attention as an adult, for another reason too. The child will have developed an anti-social, non-compliant self-concept and it must continue to elicit admonishment to maintain it. It would not know how to live with a compliant and conformist self-concept. This is known as maintaining **stroke balance**.

KNOWING WHAT WE CAN DO

OK, so we know what's wrong, but what can we do about it?

Recognising the problem
The first step is to recognise the problem and the cause underlying it. Knowledge is power. Some typical problems, together with underlying causes, are listed in Figure 1. Do any of these apply to you?

Where feelings are the problem

Be ready for it
Get to know the situations in which the problems are most likely to occur. Acknowledge the likelihood of contamination, exclusion and /or internal dialogue. Resolve to over-ride their effect.

Over-riding the problem data
Whenever a vulnerable situation arises – e.g. an interview, a question of delegation, a need to give orders, a general feeling of not

Problem	Underlying cause/s
Not being able to cope as you should	Internal dialogue
Unjustified self-doubts	Contamination by natural child
Constantly attracting negative attention	Contamination by adaptive child
Feelings of inferiority	Contamination by natural child
Constant, apparent bad luck	Contamination by natural/adaptive child
Compulsive gambling	Contamination by natural child and, perhaps, also adapted child
Accident proneness	Contamination by adapted child
Choosing and living with violent partner/s	Contamination by adapted child and/or parent
Being the one everyone puts upon	Contamination by nurturing parent
Being anti-social, rebellious	Exclusion of critical parent and/or contamination by adapted child
Not being able to conform	Exclusion of critical parent and/or contamination by adapted child
Being unable to delegate	Contamination by nurturing parent
Being unpopular because of inflexibility and narrow outlook	Exclusion of adult and both facets of child. Perhaps, also, contamination by critical parent
Having no sense of humour, or fun	Exclusion of natural child
Inability to persevere, or concentrate on a task	Exclusion of parent (both types)
Inability to control morality of behaviour	Exclusion of critical parent
Insensitivity and inability to sympathise	Exclusion of nurturing parent
Inability to give orders	Exclusion of critical parent.

Fig. 1. Typical problems that can block potential.

being able to cope, or an urge to gamble – this is what to do. Mentally switch off the child and parent parts of your mind, so that you are using the adult part. You will be doing this if you stick to purely rational thought only. Allow no hunches, feelings or vague reservations to influence you. Only one of the three parts can be dominant at any one time so if you decide to use the purely rational, adult part the others will be subordinated.

Their influence will probably impinge, tempting you to take irrational feelings and guilt data into account, but you have to feel the discomfort and carry on. You have to rigorously and totally override them – no half measures.

Utilising the mind–body consistency
If you behave as if you have particular feelings about yourself those feelings will follow. Likewise, if you behave as if you do not have feelings that limit you, those feelings will cease to be there. This is because our mind/body system demands that a consistency will develop between our behaviour, our thoughts and feelings. We may not be able to directly control our feelings very well, but with will-power we can control our behaviour and our thoughts. Feelings will then fall into line with what we want them to be. So think and act as though those feelings which hold you back are not there.

The new feelings will be stored and later relived in similar situations. More and more you'll store success and approval data with this type of event. The more of this type of data stored the more easy the situations will be to handle. More and more you'll feel liberated from the historical forces which shaped you.

> **Dwell on your successes, not your failures. Be proud of them. Keep your successful responses close to the surface of your consciousness. This should help make the feelings they evoke take precedence over the inappropriate feelings stored long ago.**

Where action or inaction is the problem

Be ready for it
What are the courses of action which have repeatedly hindered the fulfilment of your aims? Typical kinds of self-defeating behaviour are:

• setting impossible goals

- falling for 'Get Rich Quick' schemes, which contain the seeds of inevitable disappointment

- missing opportunities

- trusting other people's judgement more than your own

- repeatedly choosing or returning to violent partners.

Before a truly rational person takes any course of action they weigh things up rationally. Here are some of the tactics of rational (adult)and non-rational (child or parent) responses:

Child and adult responses

Child	Adult
Prejudice	Rational information gathering
Guesswork	Analysis
Doubts	Conclusion and decision based upon analysis
Hopes	Plans

Whenever you have decisions or plans to make, of the kind which you normally live to regret, mentally switch off the child and parent parts of your mind and use only the adult part. Remember the adult part is the purely rational part. Yield to no hunches, vague doubts, or wishes. If child or parent data impinges – threatening your effective performance, making you doubt yourself, making you fear a mistake – rigorously and totally over-ride it. Do the thing you set out to do and let nothing in your head, or your heart stop you. Do the thing you dare not do, but which you feel you ought.

Thinking like a robot
Think like a robot as you do so. A robot would have no guilt, wishes, fears, or other feelings to limit it. It would be programmed to act simply according to rational rules. You need your parent and child parts of the psyche most of the time in order to be human and social. You don't need them, though, when you are repairing damage in your conditioning. If what you have decided is justifiable, you need have no guilt, or nagging doubts as to the appropriateness of your course of action. You need not feel it is selfish, greedy, presumptuous, or whatever.

　　You are cutting new grooves, this is the purpose. Afterwards, you'll have two sets of data – two responses to choose from – rather than just one. You'll have the old set, which blunted your actions, and the new set, which didn't. Dwell on the new response and more and more it will become your automatic one.

Here are a few simple examples of rational approaches:

Missed opportunities
You are reluctant to act positively on your judgement of a good opportunity. It appears to be a risk worth taking. You've been down this road several times before and each time ended up kicking yourself for missing the opportunity. The mere fact that other people don't take up the opportunity is not a sign that it's not a good proposition. It may be an explanation of why they stay poor. If your own careful judgement has told you that the opportunity is worth taking then blow the others, act on it. If you never try for success you will never achieve it. Letting fear of failure prevent you is like walking into the gutter to avoid falling there.

Setting impossible goals
If you normally fail to fulfil your plans, ask yourself whether the goals you are setting yourself are realistic? Think about it like this. Imagine you are someone else assessing the feasibility of your aims. Suppose that person is precluded from taking into account anything you tell them, and has to base their judgement entirely upon your observable qualities, qualifications, resources and behaviour. Do a written inventory of what you need in these respects and what you have.

Get rich quick schemes
Before you embark on a get rich quick scheme, consider the whole proposition without any salesman in the picture. Seek out others who have joined the company or scheme. Find out how things turned out for them. Do a cash-flow and break-even analysis. Assess the competition carefully. Do some formal investment appraisal calculations.

SUMMARY

- Sometimes behaviour is self-defeating.

- The causes are rooted in memory.

- Storage of experiences results in a psyche with three main parts.

- Sometimes things go wrong in the process.

- The results can be seen in self-defeating behaviour.

- The first step to correcting it is to recognise the problem and its cause.

- The second step is to over-ride the effects by using the adult part of the psyche effectively.

DISCUSSION POINTS

1. Consider a time when you have felt angry or dissatisfied with yourself. Do you recall alternating between excusing yourself and mentally kicking yourself? How long did this go on for? How unpleasant was it? What did it achieve?

2. Have you ever kicked yourself for passing up an opportunity? Did it make sense to take up the opportunity? If so, why did you decline?

3. Can you think of anyone whose behaviour can be explained in terms of *internal dialogue*, *contamination* or *exclusion*? That person might be someone known personally to you, or a character in a book, a film, or a TV series.

2
Cognitive Restructuring

ADDRESSING PROBLEMS AT A RATIONAL LEVEL

The previous chapter looked at the origins of self-defeating behaviour and at how we can address these. This chapter looks at how the process works at a conceptual level and how we can make corrections at this level.

Cognitive restructuring refers to a way of dealing with a problem where what are seen as acceptable solutions, or outcomes, cannot reasonably be expected. If the conditions cannot be changed then the only way forward is to change your conceptualisation of them and your own relation to them. This may mean lowering your expectations in some cases.

Borrowing a technique

Cognitive restructuring was designed as a therapy for anxiety and depression. However, there is no reason why it cannot be used in a self-help way, for personal growth and development.

The effects are not very long lasting when administered by a therapist, but there are grounds for not generalising this to a self-help situation. Cognitive restructuring depends entirely on **rationality**. It is often pointed out that rational argument alone is not a very strong means of attitude change. However, when this claim is made it refers to changing attitudes in a social context, that is, changing the attitudes of others who have no prior wish to change them. While therapy sessions are social situations, self-help situations are not. Furthermore, here, people do wish to change their responses and attitudes. This is the whole point of self-help of this kind. The very notion implies acceptance of the inappropriateness of current responses.

Cognitive restructuring does not involve direct access to the subconscious and it is at this level that maladaptive behaviour has to change. What this method can do, though, is to draw conscious attention to errors of thinking. Other methods, such as *neuro-linguistic programming* and *positive thinking*, can then be used to educate the subconscious accordingly.

BEING FREE TO CHANGE

Cognitive restructuring assumes people are free to change if they want to. It also assumes actions and feelings are simply the subjective interpretations of sense impressions. Such interpretations may be inappropriate.

Spotting inappropriate thinking

Lack of confidence, for example, is fuelled by social feedback interpreted in a particular way. Eliciting evidence of success (whether social or occupational) may lead the individual to interpret the feedback quite differently.

The previous chapter introduced the different kinds of responses the various parts of the psyche would have to the same phenomena. A recognition of this provides a crucial means of reconciliation to intolerable situations. As is always the case with the cognitive reconstruction approach, the adjustment is made not to the situation, but to our conceptualisation of it.

The child in us

As was pointed out in the previous chapter, we still carry the *child* part of us around in our psyche. When we were children things were simple and primitive. Things were either one thing or another. There were no shades of grey. Either you were good or you were bad, your mother liked you or she didn't, and so on.

Adult thinking

As adults, we know things are not quite so simple as that. We may be good in some ways, but not in others, and good at some times but not all. We may be good with some people, but not others. Some people might dislike us, but others like us. Some might like us in some ways, but not others. They may even be jealous of us, because they know others do like us. We may be out of favour at a particular moment, because of something we have done, but the feeling will not last. So the possibilities go on. The trouble is that when we feel paranoid the child part of us is in the driving seat (see page 14).

Dichotomous thinking
Irrational behaviour is the domain of the child within. When the child part of us is at the helm we use the same primitive, dichotomous thinking that we used when we were infants. They either like us or they don't, and the signals we are receiving say they don't. Then we generalise. It means everybody feels the same way, in all situations. When we allow the child part of us to take the reins we do not make the fine distinctions that an adult does.

Adaptive thinking
When this happens to you, recognise the problem and invoke the adult. That means ceasing to think in the simplistic, child way and using the fine analysis that adults are able to use instead:

> 'He doesn't like me, but that doesn't mean everybody feels the same. Furthermore, he has his own reasons for not liking me. It may be because many others do like me, but not him. He may be jealous, or feel socially intimidated by me. It may just be something I've done to annoy him. He'll feel different tomorrow. It may even be that he has just got out of the wrong side of the bed.'

TAKING THE CRUCIAL STEPS TO CORRECTION

Three crucial stages to correcting errors of thinking are:

1. Recognising that the thinking is maladaptive.
2. Searching for and identifying potential errors of thinking.
3. Testing them.

Change or rethink
If, on testing, you find your conceptualisation of the situation is justified, the way round the problem will be to prepare to come to terms with it.

Example 1
Karen was a young mother suffering from anorexia nervosa. She had been trying to emulate the achievement levels of other members of her family, but couldn't. This was the cause of her illness. I explained to her that the goal she had been setting herself was unreasonable. Her brother and sister had not had children to look after, as she had, when they were studying. I persuaded her to

restructure her expectations and accept that a goal half of what they had achieved would be just as acceptable and meritworthy in the circumstances.

Example 2
Roger had spent months grieving over the break-up of his marriage, all the time trying to find a way to repair it. It was never going to work, though. There were obstacles which could not be removed. The only way forward, in the end, was to accept that, in many ways, he would be better off without his former wife.

Example 3
Maladaptive behaviour may not present a major problem for the parties involved until some crisis in life prevents them carrying on as normal.

John and Alison were a couple who had to pretend they were not living together in order to appease Alison's parents, who had said they would never let her go home again if she remained with John. But Alison was in love with John and wanted to stay with him. She was an only child, though, and afraid of being rejected by her parents.

It did not really cause a major problem until one day Alison's mother discovered they were living together. It caused a terrible rift in the family and Alison was forced to choose between John and her parents. She chose her parents, but found it difficult to face the break-up with the one she loved.

Alison had completely restructured her conceptualisation of her need for John. To reinforce her restructuring she had thrown herself into her work and used memory blocking strategies to prevent having to face the truth of what she was losing.

She could, alternatively, have restructured her beliefs about her parents' resolve. After all, they had threatened the same before and she had stood up to them. They had not banished her from the family home at all.

One day her parents will not be there any more and then she will be alone. If she had chosen the other route, she would have had the best of both worlds. She had ignored evidence from the past.

SUMMARY

- If you find you cannot change the situation, change your own conceptualisation of, and adaptation to, it.

- Cognitive restructuring is a technique borrowed from psychotherapy.

- Changes made by this method need anchoring using other methods like neuro-linguistic programming or positive thinking.

- We are free to change if we have the courage.

- The crucial steps to change are recognising the maladaption and searching for, and testing, suspect thinking.

DISCUSSION POINTS

1. Can you think of a recent situation where the child part of your psyche was driving your responses?

2. If you were to experience that situation again, how would you 'invoke the adult'?

3
Managing Comfort Zones

REMOVING FALSE BARRIERS

People often feel there are barriers preventing them behaving successfully in particular situations. Those barriers are more often than not self-imposed, though other people will, undoubtedly, have had a hand in guiding their development.

There will be many assumptions and beliefs you hold about yourself and your opportunities. Some of them will be limiting in their nature. They may not be justified, however. Even if they ever were, they may not be justified in the present context. You should examine the situation for yourself. Other people's guidance limits the way we see things. Challenge all negative things people say about you. Consider why they are saying them. Ask: 'What's in it for them? What assumptions are they making?'

> **Sometimes it is our self image which provides the barriers.**

Our conditioning from our experiences in life has shaped our self image, i.e. our attitudes, beliefs, expectations and opinions about ourselves. These have been stored in the subconscious level of our minds. The latter makes us behave as we see ourselves to be.

Bringing your self image into your consciousness
Examine how you picture yourself. In the spaces provided, describe yourself:

Physically   _____

Mentally   _____

Educationally   _____

Socially   _____

What, in your opinion, are your strengths and weaknesses?

	Strengths	**Weaknesses**
physically	_____	_____
mentally	_____	_____
educationally	_____	_____
socially	_____	_____

Bringing the influences on your life into consciousness

- List some of the barriers you have put up for yourself.

- List some of the people who are responsible for your limiting thinking.

- List some of the people who have empowered your positive thinking.

- List any past events and traumas which are likely to be responsible for present, limiting thinking?

Now examine the validity of the beliefs involved in your listings and descriptions. Try to be objective, as if you were a different person examining them.

Understanding comfort zones

Our self image determines the degree of comfort we will have in particular situations. We will be relaxed and comfortable, free of stress only if we are in our **comfort zone**. Our comfort zone is all those situations in which we can operate according to, or close to, our self image. Our minds tell us we are out of our depth, or slumming it, and make us feel uncomfortable if the situation we are in is inconsistent with our self image.

Changing comfort zones

We can change our self image to make it appropriate for new situations in which we want to be involved.

Bringing your comfort zone data into consciousness

List your comfort zone situations. List your non-comfort zone situations. List any situations in which you want to feel comfortable, but at present do not.

Motivating yourself
You have to make yourself really want the situation you seek to add to your comfort zone.

Creating dissatisfaction
Create dissatisfaction with the parameters of your current comfort zone. Build the desire to extend it.

Bringing your level of satisfaction into consciousness
Examine your levels of satisfaction in terms of:

- career

- personal

- social

- physical

- mental

- educational

- relationships.

If our self image determines our comfort zone, then if we want to change or extend the latter we have to change our self image. We can do this by re-educating our subconscious.

TEACHING THE SUBCONSCIOUS

The way to teach the subconscious is by **conditioning**. By duping the subconscious into believing you are already in it, the situation that your conscious efforts lead you into will have been prepared as a comfort zone. Thus, it will feel inviting and you will feel comfortable enough to remain in it.
  Follow these three steps to teach your subconscious:

1. Clearly state the problem, or area of dissatisfaction.
2. Clearly state the goal.
3. Affirm the goal as if it has already been achieved, for example, 'I am quite confident enough to sing in public'. Imagine yourself confidently doing so. Describe the feeling to yourself.

Following through
If you start to feel uncomfortable, flick back to the feelings of success you had in *any* previous situation, then back to the present one.

TAKING RESPONSIBILITY FOR YOUR OWN DESTINY

As has already been said, we have to be motivated to extend our comfort zone. The more you take responsibility for the outcomes of your plans the more motivated you will be.

Positive motivation
Motivation can be positive or negative. Selecting the right type will have important consequences for the outcomes of your aims and plans.

Constructive motivation
Constructive motivation comes from analysing what we want and why we want it.

Restrictive motivation
Restrictive motivation comes from awareness of what we *have to* do. An example is revising for examinations.

Restrictive motivation leads to creative avoidance, procrastination, resentment, negative feeling and passing the blame. The locus of control is with others. Taking responsibility for your outcomes is important for this reason. It substitutes restrictive motivation with constructive motivation.

How free are you?
Analyse the things you *have to* do in your life. Do you really have to if you think about it? If you feel you have to do things, ask *why*? Remember, everyone is free to do most things.

WRITING YOUR FUTURE

Set yourself clear goals and picture them as you do so. Write each goal down in one sentence using first person narrative and present tense. Read it back to yourself and picture it being achieved in every detail. Remember that your subconscious cannot tell the difference between real and imagined data. Therefore, the positive feelings you are storing as you imagine your goal being achieved will be relived on the way to achieving it in real life.

Cognitive dissonance can work in your favour

The difference between your conceptualisation of your present situation and the newly imprinted, desired one will result in a drive for reduction. Providing you make sure the movement is away from your present, unacceptable situation, towards the desired one, the **dissonance** effect should work in your favour. To understand this effect just think what happens when you are hungry. The gap between your conceptualisation of your present state (hungry) and that of your ideal state (not hungry) leads you to find some food. That's how the dissonance effect works, by reducing the gap between the two states.

Planning in detail

Think clearly about some of the things you want for yourself. Set time limits for achieving them. Lay down some goals for different periods of your life, during the next five years. Consider the next twelve months as the short term, the second and third year as the medium term and the fourth and fifth year as the long term.

Taking every dimension into account
Plan your future in terms of the following aspects:

- personal
- educational
- physical
- relationships
- financial
- reputation
- family.

Looking for trade-offs
Look to see whether you can achieve any trade-off effects, i.e. whether setting goals in one area will help you with achievement of goals in another.

Checking for internal conflicts
Check that your goals are not conflicting or mutually hindering in any cases.

Keeping your affirmations within reach

Write your affirmations on cards and keep them with you. Where you have goals of personal development, such as developing confidence, affirm them to yourself at least twice a day. Affirm them as if you have already achieved them, i.e. as if you are already a confident person. Include every detail in your affirmations, using all the senses and sub-modalities (see page 40). Feel the emotions you ought to feel when you have achieved those personal development goals.

Keeping your own counsel

Listen to yourself primarily, not others. Keep your own counsel. Others will try to put you off developing yourself, because they themselves are not doing so. Take control of, and responsibility for, your own mind, life and destiny.

SUMMARY

- We often set up false barriers.

- Such false barriers have various origins.

- We need to bring them into our consciousness.

- Our comfort zones limit us, but we can change them.

- Constructive motivation is preferable to restrictive motivation.

- To change and develop you need to set your goals clearly and plan carefully.

- Imagine yourself in the new situation you desire.

DISCUSSION POINTS

1. Prior to reading this book were there barriers which prevented you fulfilling your desires? If so, what were they? Did they stand up to scrutiny, or were they false?

2. Are there situations in which you feel comfortable and others in which you don't? Would you like to feel comfortable in situations which are uncomfortable to you at present?

4
Using Neuro-Linguistic Programming

If what has been said so far seems too navel gazing for you, here's a more practical approach.

MANAGING OUR STATES OF MIND

One of the main things that influence whether we succeed or fail at anything is our **state of mind**. Have you noticed how sometimes you simply know that you are going to succeed at something? You know you are going to be masterful and handle the situation well – and you do? At other times, you are unconfident and it doesn't go well at all. The difference is all to do with states of mind.

Some states of mind are **enabling** and some are **limiting**. If we could manage our states of mind we could succeed and be masterful all the time.

Well, we can. First we have to know something about the nature of states of mind.

As well as states of mind influencing our experience, the reverse is also true. Experiences trigger particular states of mind. If you have always played good badminton when the match has been at a certain club, then future venues at that club will trigger a winning state of mind. If you have had success chatting up a member of the opposite sex when you have been wearing particular clothes, then those clothes will put you in a state of mind where you will expect success.

Understanding the nature of states
There are **desirable**, **undesirable** and **baseline** states. Baseline states are default states. They are the state to which you naturally tend to return.

Then there are first-aid states. When someone is distressed or downhearted, friends often advise them to pull themselves together, shake themselves, or get a grip of themselves. What they are really saying, without realising it, is 'invoke a first-aid state to see you through the night' (or day as the case may be). That is all it will achieve, though. First-aid states just provide first-aid; they will not mend the damage. Other methods such as the behaviour modification and/or cognitive restructuring strategies dealt with in this book will be necessary to achieve that.

Sometimes states of mind which originated in the past, and have no direct relevance to the present, continue to affect us negatively. We need to recognise those states as obsolete and guard against their entrapment of us. We can do this by refusing to associate our current thinking with any facts or ideas which belong in those states. More advice will be given on this later in this chapter.

Collecting positive states

Build for yourself a collection of desired states. As you learn to control your life so that your states of mind are increasingly positive, reflect on them and add them to your collection.

Analyse your successful states carefully. This will help you focus on things which will trigger the states you want to be in.

Think carefully about any times in your life when you were particularly effective in whatever you were doing. Perhaps there was a time when you were negotiating something and felt on tiptop form. Perhaps there was a job interview where you felt completely in control of the situation.

Analyse what seemed to characterise these states. It may have been that your ego was working quietly and inconspicuously, so that no internal dialogue was competing for your attention. A relatively large proportion of your mental energy was, thus, free for conscious interaction. Whatever it was that seemed to characterise that **superstate**, regard it as your **congruence signal**. This represents your peak performance state, a state which you should aim to be able to enter at will whenever you need to.

Recognising a typically negative state

The converse situation is when you have felt that absolutely nothing was going right in a situation. Your ego may have been working loudly and conspicuously, so that an internal dialogue (auditory or visual) was distracting much of your attention. This may have left you relatively unaware of the impression you were making, or even of your own tone of voice. If this, or any other, characteristic seemed paramount in your recollections of your 'worst states', then regard it as your **incongruence signal**.

Entering and exiting states at will

Practise going back into the **superstate** you identified by concentrating on the congruence signal. Practise exiting it, too, and reverting to your original state of mind.

Distinguishing between associated and disassociated states

There are associated and disassociated states. **Associated states** are those which involve the here and now, where the whole of your ego is centrally focused.

Disassociated states involve a kind of mental disengagement. Only a part of the psyche is experiencing them and the full quality of the experience, in all its facets, is not felt. Consequently, disassociated states may often be easier to deal with when high levels of negative emotion are involved. Indeed, clinical depression is one kind of disassociated state. Because the sufferer is disengaged, to some degree, from their experience, they do not feel the full effect of the emotions involved.

That is not to say that all disassociated states are negative. Sometimes it is useful to try to analyse a painful situation rationally, while trying to keep the emotive elements at bay. Disassociation can, thus, enable us to deal with and learn from painful thoughts and memories.

You can train yourself to navigate between associative and disassociative states at will.

Dealing with trances

Trances are naturally occurring states: daydreaming is an example. Trances can be shared. The most extreme forms are stage hypnotism, the collective trances invoked in spiritualist endeavours and the states in which some of the American evangelical church sects evoke in their congregations. At a less extreme level, when several people are watching the same film, at the cinema, or on the television, they are in a collective trance. To an even lesser degree, when somebody is telling a story at the bar of their local pub those listening are in a mild collective trance.

Trances can invade consciousness when you don't want them to. If this happens, avoid being trapped in them – don't associate your thinking with any of the ideas belonging to the trance. If you do so, inadvertently, then you should consciously recognise the trance and remove yourself from it.

Such states have physiological signs: just watch people who appear to be daydreaming and you will see them.

ALTERING EXPERIENCE

We can alter our states of mind if we can alter our experience, but can we do that at will? To some degree, yes. We can do it by manipulating the structural elements. These are:

- perceptual selection (known as perceptual set)
- modalities and sub-modalities
- representation systems.

Let's look closely at what experience is. It's not external events we respond to, it's their reflection in our minds. Perhaps *reflection* is not the most appropriate word, because they are not represented exactly as they are in the real world. The term psychologists use is **perception**.

Understanding the role of perception

We do not see all the detail in front of our eyes, nor do we hear all the sounds, nor smell all the smells. If our senses transmitted to our brains every single detail there was, our brains would soon overload. We have perceptual gatekeepers to select what is important, based on our assumptions, values and beliefs. In addition to selecting what to attend to, there are also three important perceptual gatekeepers which limit and modify what we do focus upon. They are:

1. Deletion.
2. Distortion.
3. Generalisation.

Deleting

We delete things to avoid **channel overload** and to enable us to take the material in quickly. We notice and respond to certain aspects and details, but not all. We do not need to attend to everything in a situation if we can get a pretty good idea of its meaning by attending to just a few. Other people's selections might be quite different.

Some people delete from experience more than others. We tend to see those people as capable of extracting the essence, or principles, from a set of circumstances more quickly than most. The more highly intelligent the person the more likely they are to do this. Deleters are **thought-leapers**.

Distorting

Because of the way our minds work we would not be able to function without **distorting** what we see and hear. In fact, we furnish our inner world by distorting what comes in through our senses. We do it to make it fit more closely with images we have stored in our heads. We then distort our stored images themselves to complete the final fit.

Distortion can hinder our comprehension, however, if it is inappropriate. Sometimes we may distort inappropriately because of inadequate learning or conditioning. We may do it deliberately to protect our ego. 'There is none so blind as those who will not see', as the saying goes. At times people distort things inappropriately in order to give them evidence of something they want to believe.

Some people tend to distort experience significantly more then others. Such individuals might be viewed as habitual **link-makers**.

Generalising

We **generalise**, too. We think because other situations of this type have these, or those, qualities, this one will too. We tend to generalise about facts, so that we don't have to think too much. It is a shortcut to understanding, but it is not always reliable. Sometimes what we have generalised about does not fit the rule. Sometimes it is one of the few cases which are different.

Some people tend to generalise more than others. Habitual generalisers tend to be dogmatic, rule ridden and narrow in their thinking. Things are either one thing or the other, never in between. Habitual generalisers tend to be prejudiced to all minority groups and tend to exhibit **authoritarian personalities**.

Controlling the gatekeepers

We can change our current experience of something by refraining from deleting and distorting the things we normally would, or by refusing to generalise. Similarly, we can redefine stored experiences by considering the deletions, distortions and generalisations they contain. We can ask ourselves whether they are all justified.

Understanding modalities and sub-modalities

Experience can be split into modalities and sub-modalities. **Modalities** are the essential building blocks. **Sub-modalities** are the qualities they possess. Suppose the experience was a meal for two. One of the modalities might be the restaurant. The sub-modalities of this would include: large/small, warm/cold, bright/dim, and so

ndividuals who have learnt to navigate mind states will be spared this
imiting experience and be free to present themselves at their best.

There are also **physiological** modalities. Rhythmic body move-
nents which indicate an emotionally charged or kinaesthetic state
night be seen in fast, slow or medium tempo, or in varying degrees
of actual movement.

UNDERSTANDING THE FIVE REPRESENTATION SYSTEMS

t's not external reality that we respond to, it's our internal
epresentation of it. We represent external reality in our heads by
neans of mentally:

• seeing (visual)

• hearing (auditory)

• tasting (gustatory)

• smelling (olfactory)

• feeling (kinaesthetic).

Not only does the outer world influence the inner world, but it's the
ame the other way round. The way we experience something in our
neads influences, in turn, the things we focus upon in the outer
world and the way we will interpret them.

Some of our experiences are highly visual and others are highly
auditory. In some the feelings are most prominent, while in others it
nay be the smell or taste that is paramount. Everyone has a
avourite, natural representation system. It is used to access stored
knowledge, like a file opener in a computer program. This is known
as their **lead system**.

Once opened, the store will reveal visual, auditory, kinaesthetic,
gustatory and olfactory details. Once it has been accessed by one
ense the contents will be experienced by the other senses.

It is this inner representation of a situation, this perception, that
we respond to. We can't change what is really out there in the world,
but we can change the way we represent it within.

Knowing your own personal representation system

Different representation systems lead to different ways of expressing
things. People whose kinaesthetic (feeling) system, for example, is the
dominant means of representing the external world in their heads will

on. The second modality would be the person you are shar
meal with. The sub-modalities would include: male/femal
average, attractive/unattractive, friendly/unfriendly, relaxec
black haired/brown haired/blonde haired, etc. A third m
would be the meal. The sub-modalities of this would i
abundant/frugal, hot/cold, tasty/bland and exotic/plain.

Sub-modalities
Sub-modalities can be categorised in terms of five represe
systems (see page 42). They are:

- visual

- auditory

- kinaesthetic

- olfactory

- gustatory.

Examples of sub-modalities in the **visual** representation
include: large/small, light/dark and red/green/blue/yellow,
the **auditory** system you find things like: loud/soft, high
medium pitched/low pitched, etc. **Kinaesthetic** sub-m
include: hard/soft, sharp/blunt and cold/warm/hot. In the
category there are things like: pleasant/unpleasant, stror
and so on. The main **gustatory** submodalities are: sweet, sou
and savoury.

Some sub-modalities play a critical role in determii
essence of an experience. If these are changed it woulc
powerful effect on our inner world.

I would not go so far as saying you should distort you
experience by changing the sub-modalities. However, the
reason why you should not attend to a different selection
present in a current experience, if the usual ones trigger a
state of mind.

A typical example is an interview situation. Perhaps your e:
to date has led you to expect oppressive panel members, whc
you a hard time. Invariably, however, interview panels conta:
one friendly member. It is a certainty they will not all b
oppressive. Pick out the one you think is the most frie
sympathetic and focus upon him or her.

Most people will be trapped in a focus upon the oppres:

tend to react relatively slowly to things. This is because emotions work slowly. It is useful to assess what is the predominant representation system which you, yourself use, i.e. your lead system. You can expand your mind by concentrating on the lesser used ones.

Knowing the physiology of representational systems

Each representation system has its own outward signs. When a visual representation system is predominantly in evidence, the face tends to be tilted upwards. Breathing tends to be short and shallow. When an auditory representation system is predominating, body movements tend to be rhythmic. There may be actual, or silent speech. By the latter, I mean there may be movements of the mouth, suggestive of speech. The head may be cocked on one side. When a kinaesthetic representation system is the more powerful at a particular moment in time, the individual will adopt a slumped, more rounded posture. They will also tend to look down, speak in a deep voice and their breathing will tend to be rather slow and abdominal in nature.

Individual differences in understandings and perceptions can often be explained in terms of differences in lead systems.

Managing our perceptual set

That is not to say we should deliberately, or even undeliberately, see it other than it really is. It is, rather, to say we can change the limited selection of aspects and details to attend to. We cannot attend to them all, we would overload, so we select what we see as most relevant. It is not the only selection which we can make, indeed, others will see different priorities to us. It is not distorting the perception by doing this, it's already a distorted image of the real world. If anything, it amounts to changing one distortion for a more useful or a less limiting one.

Changing our representational systems

If we are in a situation which would normally be associated with a negative state of mind, we can change our experience of it. We can do this by changing the representation system we are using. If the limiting state of affairs we have stored in our mind is a relatively visual one, we can try attending to the present circumstances in a rather verbal way, or kinaesthetic way. The experience we are having will then cease to be a limiting one based on an inappropriate state of mind.

Using physiological handles

As has been said, these representation systems have physiological aspects. Once we know them, we can change our physiological behaviour, so that it is no longer appropriate for the representation system keeping us in an unwanted state.

Controlling internal dialogues

For example, one of the most limiting experiences is an **internal dialogue** (see page 17). Internal dialogues are situations where two parts of the psyche are disagreeing. First we think we should do something, then we think we shouldn't and then we think we should again. We cannot make up our mind. Sometimes it refers to an alternation between self-blame and self-excuse. Sometimes it refers to a course of action not yet taken. It may run like this:

Oh, how stupid I have been!
But how could I have known?
But I should have known!
Anyone can make a mistake.

Alternatively, it might run like this:

I've decided I will take the new job.
But, Oh, I'm not really sure.
Yes, I am sure.
I wonder if I'm doing the right thing.

We continue oscillating, getting nowhere, until we feel stressed, weary and depressed.

Internal dialogues obviously rely on an auditory representation system. Physiological counterparts of this are a tilted head, possibly body swaying, and the direction of gaze may be level or down to the left. When a visual representation system is in use, the direction of gaze will be upwards, or level, with breathing being short and high in the chest. Visual representation systems cannot support an internal dialogue. By changing your physiological behaviour you can, therefore, help to end your internal dialogue and change your state of mind.

Preventing unwanted habitual thoughts

If you tend to be troubled by habitual thoughts that you do not want to have, you can prevent them in the following way. Identify the representation system chiefly responsible for producing those thoughts. Identify the physiological handles (outward signs) of that representation system. Cancel the operation of that representation system by changing your physiological behaviour to that which represents a different one.

Depression impairs right hemisphere functioning, therefore the left hemisphere of the brain becomes most active. The left hemisphere is the side of the brain involved in sequential processing. Consequently, it is there where language is produced and understood. Because of this, the auditory representation system plays a dominant role in thinking. People who are depressed are not forward thinking, but dwell on the present and the past. An outward sign which you would expect of this state of mind would be a tendency to gaze downwards and to the right. Deliberately adjusting their posture should help them change their state of depression. Tilting the head up and gazing upwards and to the right is a posture inconsistent with depression. This will not be enough, in itself, for a state of depression involves a chemical imbalance, too. Furthermore, it is an emotional response and emotions change relatively slowly. Nevertheless, it is a start. With positive thinking and determination most people should be able to go on to shift a state of depression.

Interacting with others

Understanding representation systems can be useful in interacting with others. Have you noticed how support you offer when a friend has a problem sometimes tends to be spurned? At times, your well-meaning intervention appears to be making matters even worse. It may be that you have not supported them in the right way. You may not have used the representation systems with which they represent their problems in their minds. You have to try to assess and mirror the representation systems that are involved in their definition of their problem. Fortunately, friends tend to have common preferred representation systems. This is why they tend to be generally supportive of each other.

CHANGING ASSUMPTIONS, VALUES AND BELIEFS

Other things which affect our experience are: the assumptions we make, our values and our beliefs.

Values

If we believe in film censorship we will experience a violent film differently from the way we would experience it if we held anti-censorship values.

Beliefs

If we believe our partners will always be faithful to us, we will experience a conspicuous flirtation differently to the way we would if we did not hold such a belief.

Making assumptions

When we comprehend any event we use our powers of reasoning and comparison to arrive at our understanding. We are not able to analyse everything down to the last detail, though. We would never come to any conclusion at all if we did not draw the line somewhere and take some things for granted. We would have to trace every individual thought back to infinity, uncovering grounds and proving them at every stage of the way.

Everyone has to make assumptions, but some assumptions may be unjustified and it may be those which prevent us thinking in a successful way. Indeed, problem solving can be regarded as having a task which is impossible on the present assumptions. What is necessary is to find which of the assumptions can be changed.

Example 1

Consider a group of soldiers under attack. They may decide it is best to stay put until they are rescued by helicopter, rather than try to escape on foot. They know a helicopter has been despatched. What they are assuming, though, but don't know for certain, is that the helicopter has not crashed.

Example 2

Another example might be where a man sees an attractive woman in a night-club. He is about to approach her and introduce himself, when another man joins her. He then changes his mind. The man has made the assumption that the man who joined her is her husband or boyfriend. However, that assumption may be wrong: it may be her brother, or simply a friend.

Sometimes we find ourselves in double binds – we are damned if we do and damned if we don't do something. The assumption is that there is no third way. Perhaps that assumption is wrong.

Changing assumptions and values

If the assumptions you make are limiting you, check them out to see if they can be avoided.

Understanding the power and resilience of beliefs
Beliefs are powerful gatekeepers on perception. Sometimes they are held on very shaky grounds. Nevertheless, even dubious beliefs can be hard to shift, especially if they are centralised beliefs, or beliefs a person holds about their identity. One of the ways that beliefs can cause our perception to work against our interests is by often being self-fulfilling. They limit our perceptual set to selecting those phenomena which reinforce the beliefs themselves.

Understanding the origins of beliefs
Beliefs originate from three sources:

- modelling
- conflict
- repetition.

Many of our beliefs arise from **modelling** similar beliefs in our parents and other authority figures. These include those most central to us and most resistant to change. In our earliest years, when our centralised beliefs take root, we do not have the capability to challenge whether they are justified. Once we have internalised them, without challenge, they become firmly rooted. They become resistant to change, even in the face of evidence challenging their validity. However, just because they are difficult to change in the normal way it doesn't mean to say they cannot be changed by insightful methods.

Beliefs also originate through **conflict**. A person who has always believed the village tearaway is just misguided and high-spirited might change their belief if they are mugged by him. Similarly, an unconditional pacifist might suddenly change their belief in non-violence after being attacked.

You have probably heard the saying that if you tell somebody something often enough they will believe it. This is true, **repetition** is one of the sources from which we derive our beliefs.

Beliefs have a sub-modality structure. We will not simply believe that somebody is rich, we will believe they are reasonably rich, very rich or extremely rich.

Sharing beliefs
Many beliefs are shared with others. It is shared centralised beliefs which unite some communities, for example, religious groups. Indeed, because of the lack of tangible grounds for religious beliefs, there is always doubt about their validity. One of the ways people gain confidence that they have chosen the right belief is by knowing many others believe it. The more people believe as they do the stronger will be the belief. Consequently, the newer religious sects indulge in evangelising. This is *spreading the word*, persuading others to believe as they do.

The same goes for attitudes. The more people share a common attitude the more they will feel confident that it is justified.

Changing inappropriate beliefs
Sometimes beliefs limit your life chances while at the same time affording little utility to you or anyone else. When this is the case you need to examine them, together with your grounds for holding them. Consider whether they should be discarded or changed. If you do replace beliefs you need to be sure you replace them with appropriate ones, otherwise inappropriate ones can quickly form in the vacuum.

Aiming for belief–behaviour congruence
What you should aim for is belief–behaviour congruence. This is where the beliefs you hold are consistent with the behaviour you wish to exhibit and feel justified in doing so.

Acting out the change
One of the ways to change beliefs is to act out the change, that is to act as if the new, desired belief is true. It will not be easy. Your subconscious, which does not understand rationality, will be working against you, resisting the change. It will feel uncomfortable and, perhaps, even scary. However, if you want to change the belief, and feel you are justified in doing so, then you must accept the fear and act out the change anyway. This way the inappropriate data stored in your subconscious will gradually be replaced with appropriate data consistent with the belief. The old data will still be there, but it will be overcompensated for by the new data. When this has reached an adequate level, acting out your new belief will feel quite natural and comfortable.

Changing them a bit at a time

When you wish to change a belief, examine the sub-modalities of that belief carefully. If you have never believed you could be an effective public speaker, consider carefully in what way have you believed you would fail. You might answer in terms of organising your material, making your voice heard, refraining from stuttering and not going red. If so, focus on each one of these at a time and set sub-goals to prove to yourself otherwise. You needn't try to achieve them all at once. Try putting on a talk where somebody else has organised material and you have a microphone present. That way you need only concentrate on speaking slowly and calmly. When you have proved this to yourself, set about organising your own material and then prove that aspect to yourself too. So it goes on until you have proved to yourself that every aspect of your belief that you would not make an effective public speaker was unfounded.

Challenging normalisations and prohibitions

Normalisations

Normalisations are statements about what you ought to do. These can sometimes be limiting and may be unjustified. If you find this is so, challenge their current validity. Ask yourself what would be the consequences of not doing these things, or of doing things which you have been led to believe you ought not to do?

Prohibitions

Sometimes such limiting factors are expressed even more strongly. These are known as prohibitions. Clearly, there are some prohibitions which we must maintain in order to be human and social. There are others, however, which may not, any longer, serve a useful purpose for us or anyone else. Prohibitions may appear to be limiting you unreasonably if they don't seem to be limiting other people around you. If this is the case, challenge their current validity. Do this in the same way as has been suggested for challenging normalisations.

Avoiding misinterpretation

We are affected by what people say about us and what they say may seem negative. To avoid misinterpretation of negative feedback, however, get used to **chunking down** the message. Chunking down means segmenting something which is said and examining the sub-modalities. Suppose your boss said you were not the right person for a new job which had been created. Don't automatically interpret the message as 'my boss doesn't think very highly of me'. Ask yourself 'In what way am I not the right person? Is it that I am too young, or, too inexperienced, or do I not have the appropriate personality?' If it is the latter, he might even mean you need more challenge than that job would provide. If it is that you are too young, then your boss might feel that you are quite capable, but that he would not be able to justify it to others in the firm if he gave you the job. If you are not skilled enough, then there will come a time when you are.

LEARNING ABOUT ANCHORS

Types of anchor
There are three categories of things which can secure for you a particular state of mind. They are known as anchors. Those categories are:

1.   Role models.
2.   Physiology.
3.   Thinking of a time when you were in a desired state.

Role models can be used to anchor states of mind which you imagine such characters to have. Suppose a character in a book you have read, or a film you have seen, was particularly effective in business or in interactions with the opposite sex. You will tend to infer that they had a particular state of mind at such times. By invoking that role model in your mind you can bring into your consciousness the state of mind which you imagine they had.

Think about times when you were particularly successful in ways relevant to your present aims. You may well recall receiving praise for your successes. Praise will, thus, represent an anchor which can secure for you, again, the state of mind you had then. Focus on the praise you received and what it felt like.

Being an anchor for others
Have you ever thought that you can change other people's states of mind? You, yourself, represent an anchor for others. People will recall how they felt, or tend to commonly feel, when you are around them. If the state which you anchor in their minds is desirable they will want to associate with you. If it is undesirable, however, they will tend to avoid you. It is important, therefore, to contribute to other people's experience in ways which make it desirable.

This is an example of an external anchor. External anchors exist outside our minds, while internal anchors originate from memories.

Working with anchors

Sometimes something you see or hear will trigger unhappy memories and, with them, undesirable states of mind. If this happens rarely such obsolete anchors will not represent a major problem. However, if something you see day in day out keeps evoking painful memories, then the obsolete anchor needs to be neutralised. The way to do this is to refuse consciously to associate with the ideas belonging to the state it triggers. Instead, focus on other more positive and desirable things, making that anchor trigger, if anything, a desirable state.

Advertisers use anchors. The motor industry is a good example. Where cars are aimed at the male population, manufacturers tend to present sexy female models sitting on, or being associated in some way with, the vehicle concerned. If the advertisement is successful, the image of that car will anchor a state of mind in which males will feel sexy. This will be because male viewers of the advertisements will have associated that state of mind with a particular anchor, in this case the car.

Making anchors

You can use almost any visual image to consciously design an anchor for a state of mind. You do it like this: think yourself into the desired state of mind and imagine that visual image playing a crucial role. In this way you associate that anchor to that state.

Developing complex states

You can also experiment with blends of states of mind. It should be possible to develop complex states by associating more than one with the same anchor.

You can sharpen up the effectiveness of an anchor by inducing a state from several different anchors. This might involve using visual, auditory, kinaesthetic, olfactory and/or gustatory memories. When you are firmly in that state of mind then focus on just one particular anchor, e.g. a visual one. Practise exiting that state and entering it again using that anchor alone.

Emotional responsibility

Don't abdicate emotional responsibility yourself, and don't let others do so. Challenge any statements made which appear to blame you for emotional upsets in others. We all have a duty to give reasonable protection to those whose emotions may be hurt by our direct action. However, some people have a tendency to look for scapegoats and take no responsibility themselves at all. In any human interaction there are always at least two players and both contribute, to some degree, to the outcomes. It is important to take into account and try to protect other people's emotions from negative effects of your own interactions with them. That does not mean taking all the blame, though.

Wherever you are involved in a situation where you are being made a scapegoat, draw the other party's attention to the fact. Tell them they are using you as a scapegoat and that there were two players in the game both contributing to the outcome. Demand that they accept some emotional responsibility.

UNDERSTANDING THE ROLE OF METAPHORS

Human beings allow metaphors to guide their behaviour. These are powerful devices which do more than merely rationalise, they abstract and highlight general principles.

The metaphors people use tell you a lot about their inner world and the kind of people they are. Take notice of the metaphors people use and you will understand them better.

This works reflexively, too. Examine the metaphors you yourself use and you will gain greater self-knowledge.

In addition to metaphors, stories play an important part in the development of people's inner worlds. Not only do they enable us to share our thinking and experience with others, they enable us to store internal representations of experiences we have never actually had.

Examining your own metaphors

Think about what your own metaphors are. Which metaphors feature prominently when you are talking to people? Individuals who don't give people a second chance, for example, tend to be influenced by the 'leopard doesn't change its spots' type of metaphor. An assumption underlying this is that people are either good or bad; moral development is a fallacy. Some people often speak of 'flogging a dead horse' and 'beating your head against a brick wall'. These are the kinds of metaphors which tend to limit thinking and behaviour. An assumption underlying the first of these is that just as the death of a horse is irreversible, so are human situations. An assumption underlying the second is that some problems are absolutely insoluble. Neither of these assumptions is valid.

Make a thorough analysis of all the metaphors you tend to use in conversation. Enlist the help of a friend or family member if you like. This will certainly make things easier and the analysis more thorough. You could also do this as a group exercise with several others who want to streamline their minds.

When you have a thorough list of all the metaphors you tend to frequently use, analyse the assumptions underlying them.

Now make an honest assessment of whether your metaphors are valid and useful to you. If they are not, perhaps you should choose better ones.

Using metaphors

You can use metaphors to solve problems. Suppose you have a particularly painful problem. Construct a metaphor of it. This involves thinking of a different set of circumstances where the principles and the central problem are the same. Try to solve the metaphorical problem. Unlike your real problem, thoughts about the metaphorical problem will not be associated with painful feelings. Consequently, you should be able to think more clearly and rationally.

Metaphors can be powerful in respect of handling relationships. Describing something the other party does which upsets you, or which you think is not fair, can often arouse strong emotional reactions. This leads to counter accusations and tempers start to rise as these proliferate. In the end nothing is achieved expect bad feeling. One way round the problem is to construct a metaphor of the point you are trying to make. That should not arouse strong emotional reactions, as it is not directly personal. Try to make the other person understand and agree with the conclusions of the metaphor. If you succeed, you can then sensitively relate it to the problem you have in your relationship, which was too volatile to discuss.

ACCELERATING YOUR LEARNING

We can put our learning into a higher gear by paying attention to the way we model successful behaviour and the learning strategies we use.

Modelling

Use modelling to copy excellence in another person's behaviour. Whatever you want to achieve, identify someone who tends to achieve it easily. Study their behaviour and copy it.

What you have to do is find the essence of that behaviour. Find what it is that makes it successful. Don't limit yourself to the observable behaviour, infer the subconscious processes underlying it. Try to imagine what that person feels like as they perform that behaviour and as they achieve their successes.

When you are modelling the successful behaviour of another, do it comprehensively. Model their:

- thinking

- beliefs

- values

- behaviour.

Think what you imagine they think while they are performing the successful behaviour. Believe what you think they tend to believe.

When you learn how to model people successfully you can transfer the skills from one situation to another. Modelling skills are acting skills. When an actor learns how to act at stage school, they then use those skills to perform many different parts in the future. Each time they do this they study the behaviours of the characters they are playing and infer their inner world. Then they think themselves into the part and attempt to live those character's lives for the duration of time they are playing the roles. This is what you have to do to really successfully model achievement behaviour.

Another way to learn skills is to break the overall skill up into sub-skills. Learn each sub-skill by repetition and error correction. Finally, re-combine the sub-skills to create the overall skill.

Skills learned by modelling last longer than skills learned the other way.

Using learning strategies

Changing an unsatisfactory situation in your life can be a difficult task. Sometimes your emotions will prevent, or limit you analysing possibilities in an objective way. There are two stages to overcoming the problem.

1. Acknowledge the unsatisfactoriness of the situation.

2. Analyse the situation in a disassociated state of mind (see page 38), so that you are detached from the problem. This will protect your thinking from some of the effects of emotions. You can also make a metaphor of the problem. Ask objectively

what needs to be changed to make the situation satisfactory.

Sometimes faults in behaviour occur because of the fact that an inappropriate representation system is in operation. Suppose you find you cannot spell a word that you have always been able to spell in the past. It may be because an auditory representation system is operative. You may be a highly visual person and tend to remember spellings by what the words look like. If this is the case, try looking up instead of down and this should enable you to engage a visual representation system. This may solve the problem.

Expanding our mind through representation systems

Practise changing your inner world by means of different representation systems. This way you will expand your schemata (stored detail relating to the external world). The more complex your schemata the more curious you will become, the more knowledge you will be able to absorb and the more quickly you will be able to understand it.

By using multiple representation systems to furnish your inner world, you will facilitate learning by multiple perspective. This is very powerful.

If a state of mind which particular situations put you into is undesirable and unsuccessful it is possible to change it. Examine the sub-modalities (see page 40) of the experience you have in such situations and then make changes to those which you think give the experience a negative quality.

Another way of changing unsuccessful behaviour for more successful behaviour is simply to keep your objectives steady and vary your behaviour until you achieve success. Always judge behaviour by what it achieves.

After you learn anything – by modelling, skill dissection and repetition, disassociation, change of representation system, or change of sub-modalities – always analyse what you have learned, preferably in writing.

States and social interaction

States of mind are catching. If you are happy then others around you will be happy. If you are miserable then you will make everyone else miserable. If you want to fill your mind store with positive states of mind then it's best to avoid negative people.

You can learn to recognise states of mind in people by the physiological signs that they display. When people are habitually hunched up and gazing down to the right they are probably depressed. If their gaze is often upwards and to the right they are likely to be relatively forward looking and rather visual in their thinking. Looking down and to the left quite a lot is a sign of inner speech. Such individuals often tend to be tortured by internal dialogues.

There are also, of course, the obvious outward signs of internal states of mind. These include the smile, the frown, the tightness of jaw and the many different things that the eyes can tell us.

If you want to influence other people's states of mind you have to first pace them to neutral. Do this by mirroring their outward physiological signs and gradually changing your own behaviour to neutral. Suppose, for example, you want to get someone out of a diffident mood. Suppose they are troubling themselves with questions of: 'Should they, or shouldn't they?' Begin by gazing down and to the left just as they do and mirroring their own physiological movements. Gradually, as you are talking to them, adjust your gaze to the horizontal, to the here and now.

Alternatively, you can invoke in people particular states of mind by telling them a story which triggers the state you wish to bring about.

SETTING GOALS

The most important part of mastering your own destiny is deciding exactly what it is you want. People tend to skirt around this question. They kid themselves that they basically do know what they want, when actually they are not really sure. There are reasons why people don't set down their goals:

- fear/risk

- being reluctant to limit their spontaneity

- being afraid of liberty.

Nor is it enough to simply know what you want; you've got to clearly define it if you are to make it happen. You've got to be able to imagine it in detail. Break your goals down into elements and plan the order in which you will achieve them.

Avoiding negative goals

Avoid negative goals for they are hard to realise. Examples of these are goals to give up smoking and chocolate and to stop biting one's nails. Express them, as far as you can, in positive terms. For example, set a goal for how long you can go without a cigarette, rather than a goal for never smoking again.

Knowing where you are starting from and what you want to keep

You also need to be aware of where you are at the present. Otherwise, you will not be able to measure your effectiveness in pursuing your goals. Be sensitively aware of what your present situation gives you. Is it what you still want? Consider also the negative consequences of your goal. There may be things you will lose in the process and these may be important to you. Think how you can adjust your goals and your methods of achieving them to avoid losing what you want to keep.

Transcending present boundaries

Lastly, don't limit yourself to goals which appear feasible under present circumstances. You can change the conditions.

Planning

In addition to setting your goals, it is important to plan carefully how you are going to achieve them.

Handling time

You need to take a **through time** approach to planning. This is easier for some people than others. Some people may be regarded as *in time* people, while others tend to be *through time* people. Business people tend to be of the latter kind. 'Through time' people tend to view time running from left to right in front of their eyes. This is essential to planning their time. 'In time' people, in contrast, see time running away from them directly in front. Consequently, it is difficult for them to plan.

Associated states, as dealt with on page 38, tend to be 'in time'. This is because they take place in the here and now. Disassociated states, in contrast, are 'through time'. This is because in them, rather than experience directly, we reflect on experience, or view it from a distance. If we are not *living the time* we can view it as a whole.

Scheduling

List carefully the internal resources you will need. These include such things as money, knowledge and skill. Consider also what external resources you will need. These include the help of other people and the availability of situations which will provide you with the opportunities you need.

Harmonising your sub-goals
Ask yourself whether the goals you have set and your plans for achieving them are consistent with what might be regarded as your overall master plan of life. It's no good planning to establish yourself with a reputation and, perhaps, a place in local politics, when your main desire is extensive world travel.

What you should be aiming for is developing congruity or harmony between your different neurological levels. These are behaviour, identity, environment, beliefs, capability and spiritual aspects of your life. Incongruence is difficult to handle, it creates anxiety, saps your energy and makes you feel uncomfortable.

Get used to listening to your feelings, they are telling you important things all the time. Your feelings are the only real indicators you have of what is absolutely right for you. Don't ignore them. Aim to strike a balance between what your rational mind is telling you and what your feelings are telling you. In other words, aim for congruence between your conscious and your subconscious mind.

In your plan, you should aim to apply the techniques to **six levels** of your life:

1. Environment.
2. Behaviour.
3. Identity.
4. Beliefs.
5. Capability.
6. Spiritual.

The four stages to excellence
In your personal development you should aim to progress through four clearly defined levels of success:

1. Unconscious incompetence.
2. Conscious incompetence.
3. Conscious competence.
4. Unconscious competence

Staying in control
Plan to be personally in control as much as possible. That does not mean you should not delegate. Delegation is important if you want

to achieve more than the average individual. What is important, though, is to keep control over the crucial points in your plan. These are the stages which can make or break your achievement and which can alter the direction of your progress.

Design a checklist so that you can tick things off as you achieve them and record dates so that you can plan to make up lost time. To make the latter work you will need to arrange for fast feedback on each stage of your progress.

When mental or physical skills really come to fruition they become both competently and unconsciously produced. Consider walking, for example. If you had to think about the way you were moving your legs you would bump into a lamppost.

Metacognition

Metacognition means thinking about thinking. You can liberate yourself from faulty thinking by systematically questioning that thinking. First you need to write down the problem in as much detail as possible. For example, if internal dialogue is torturing you, then listen carefully to what your mind is, almost with a will of its own, saying to itself. Listen to the kind of ideas that it is turning over and over, accepting and then challenging. Write the dialogue down in as much detail as you can so that you can evaluate it objectively. Next, ask what is deleted from this (see page 39) and, therefore, what assumptions are being made? Are those assumptions justified? Take small sections of the written material and clarify the meaning, writing it down to crystallise it. Now look it over again objectively, on paper – dialogue and clarifications. Does it still appear the same as it did when its medium was your mind? Is it easier to handle now? Invariably, the answer will be yes.

SUMMARY

- One of the main influences on our behaviour is our state of mind.

- We can alter our state of mind if we alter our experience.

- We can alter our experience if we understand its structure.

- Experience is structured in terms of representation systems and sub-modalities.

- Experience is subject to the limitations of our perceptual set.

- Experience is influenced by our beliefs, values and assumptions.

- Experience has physical reflections which can be used as handles to change it.

- The four pillars of neuro-linguistic programming are:
  1. rapport
  2. knowing what you want
  3. being in touch with your senses
  4. being flexible in your behaviour.

- Personal development moves through four levels to excellence: from unconscious incompetence to unconscious competence.

- Attention is applied to six levels of analysis.

- A principal aim is to achieve congruity with and between these levels.

DISCUSSION POINTS

1. Think of a recent situation where you failed to achieve success. What was your state of mind at the time? What would you do now to change it?

2. Think of six beliefs you hold. Do they originate from modelling, conflict or repetition?

5
Positive Thinking

UNDERSTANDING THE ROLE OF THE SUBCONSCIOUS

This chapter deals with straightforward **positive thinking**. You might well know that you're as good as anyone else, as clever and effective at your job. You might well know you have valid grounds for believing you are attractive and desired by the opposite sex. Your rationality may tell you that you will be able to cope with any situation that is reasonably likely to confront you. However, rationality is not enough.

It's your subconscious mind which tends to limit your behaviour. It does this by causing you to relive negative feelings you have stored in similar situations.

Just because there were times when you did not respond effectively, or were rejected, it doesn't mean to say you are going to be ineffective, or rejected, in every similar situation in the future. Indeed, it doesn't mean the same has to happen in any such situation. Your subconscious does not know this, though, for it doesn't work by rationality. It works by simply storing the connections between the events and the feelings, and throwing these up to your consciousness when a similar situation arises again.

What you have to do to overcome this is re-educate the subconscious. You cannot do this by rational means, you have to do it by creating similar situations and making yourself feel positive in response. The easiest way of doing this is to simply imagine those situations and imagine yourself being accepted or liked in them. Your subconscious cannot tell the difference between reality and imagination, so the storage will be just as effective.

Our thoughts shape our future
Our thoughts shape our direction, so if we dwell on negative thoughts our direction will be negative. Think only of what you want to happen. Your thoughts become your future. Think thoughts

about what you want to happen, not what you don't want to happen. Think only good thoughts about yourself.

Choosing positive friends and associates

Model other people who are positive. Don't associate with negative people. Both positive and negative thinking are contagious. The only justifiable reason for associating with negative people is if you are helping them to change their own thinking from negative to positive.

DEALING WITH SPECIFICS

From here on, this chapter will deal with the application of positive thinking techniques to a variety of behavioural problems which people experience.

Overcoming lack of confidence

If you lack confidence it may be that you have never had it to an adequate degree. On the other hand, it may be that something has happened to make you lose it.

If you have lost your confidence

If you had confidence once you can have it again. Acknowledge what it was that made you lose it and address the problem. Think of times when you were confident and have them in mind when you are in social situations. Think like a confident person and you'll be a confident person.

Furthermore, if you think like a confident person you will appear confident and other people will seek you out. This is because people like confident people, for states of mind are contagious (see page 55). If people seek you out and want to associate with you this will reinforce your confidence further.

If you have never felt confident

If you have never felt confident then make a conscious decision to turn over a new leaf. Choose a confident role model, and act and feel like that person. The longer you keep it up the more positive data will be stored and the more that coat will fit. Remember, your subconscious cannot tell the difference between real data and fantasy data.

Imagine yourself doing something you'd be proud of. It can be the subject of a story you have read, or a film you have seen. It can simply be a daydream about what you would like to happen. Your subconscious will store the success data as if it is real and will replay it in similar, but real circumstances. Such replay will make you feel capable and confident and make you expect success.

Don't let others put you down

Your lack of confidence may be partly due to other people tending to put you down and to understate your qualities and potential. If this is the case, ask yourself why they might do it. It is likely to be to give themselves a leg up, socially speaking. They may well be using you to give themselves something (or someone) to stand on, as they themselves try to climb out of the social mire. When it happens, ask yourself: 'Why are they saying this? What's in it for them?' Compensate by talking positively to yourself.

Overcoming paranoia

Do you feel people dislike you? If so, ask yourself whether there are valid reasons why this could be true?

- Are you shy?

- Are you arrogant?

- Do you have body odour?

- Do you hog the limelight?

- Do you interrupt people?

- Do you put them down?

- Do you talk behind their back?

- Do you take the Mickey?

- Are you a whinger?

If you tend to torture yourself with the belief that people do not like you, start smiling at people and making conversation. You'll surprise yourself with the good responses you will get. Not everyone will respond positively, but most will.

Give yourself a script to say when you feel at risk of shyness. Here is an example:

People like me and want to be with me. People find me interesting and fun to be with. I like myself and others. I make friends easily. I find it easy to talk to people.

Learning to love yourself

Do you mistrust people? Do you feel they are going to let you down or hurt you? Do you feel people are talking behind your back? When people laugh, do you immediately react as if they are laughing at you? These kinds of things indicate a personal dislike of yourself and you will project this to others. As a result, they will see you as unlikeable. To like or love others, you have first got to like and love yourself.

Refusing to take criticism lying down

If you are being criticised and you do not understand why, don't just accept it or avoid it, clarify it first. Ask yourself whether it is justified. If you feel it is not, then challenge it. Stick up for yourself.

Dealing with relationships or lack of them

Dealing with loneliness

Do you suffer from loneliness? Do you spend most of your time alone? Do you find it hard to make friends? Do you find it hard to talk to people? Do you feel unhappy on your own?

There are many other, unattached people out there. They are not easy to find, but only you can do it. Furthermore, they don't know you are there and available. Instead of dwelling on their inaccessibility address the problem and seek them out. If you just dwell on your loneliness, you will always be lonely.

Dealing with a broken relationship

If you have recently been left by your partner, you will be feeling pretty bad and your ego will have been damaged. Don't suppress anger. It is this which will help you through. You have a right to be angry.

There will be another prospective partner. You've just got to find him or her.

Write yourself a script. Say something like:

> I'm not going to let this destroy me. I'm attractive and have a lot to offer. There are plenty of prospective partners out there. I just have to find them and I will.

Playing inappropriate roles

Are you a mouse?
Do people walk all over you? Do you try to appease people? Is the guiding principle of your life seeking to endear yourself to others? Will this make life good for you? Has it so far?

Sometimes this type of personality is seen as ineffectual, or even stupid. If you are tired of being walked over, change it. Say to yourself: 'I am not going to be a mouse anymore.'

Nice guys
Are you the nice guy, the guy who is reliable, a shoulder for everyone, but whom nobody wants for a partner? If so, tell yourself you have had enough of playing this role. You are no longer going to be the one on whom everyone dumps their problems.

Fearing success

Happiness and success will not come to you, you have to reach out for them. Some people realise this and do so, but then give up when they find they are having no success, or they lose their courage. Change is a little frightening, even change for the better. It involves going into territory you don't know. You are not familiar with the routes.

One of my students once told me she did not like it when things were going well. She always got the feeling that someone would come and kick her up the backside.

One approach to life is to walk into the gutter to avoid falling into it. If change is for the better – to happiness, pleasure and love – there is the chance of getting hurt. If you have just recovered from a painful relationship break-up you will be feeling lonely and thinking that you will never replace the person you lost. There will be a strong incentive to stay lonely and miserable, because at least you cannot fall any further. If you find another relationship and become happy you run the risk of repeating all the heartache again. One way to prevent falling into misery and despair is to live in it. Do you really want that, though? If you did, you would not be reading this book.

It is the same with financial or career success. It is especially the case if you have just recovered from a collapse in one or both of these areas of life, for example, bankruptcy, insolvency or redundancy. One minute you were riding high, the next you were on your behind. Dare you risk that happening again? The higher you climb, the further there is to fall.

Suffering from low self-esteem
However, when we do not achieve as highly as we believe we are capable of we suffer low self esteem. Such achievement level may refer to a career, social acceptance, financial success or success with the opposite sex, That is what low self esteem is, the measure of the gap between *ideal* and *actual* self concepts of achievement.

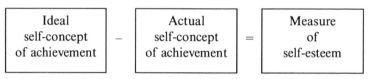

| Ideal self-concept of achievement | − | Actual self-concept of achievement | = | Measure of self-esteem |

(the smaller the gap the higher the self esteem).

Low self esteem is hard to cope with. It is a miserable state and it is continuous. The alternative – performing at your best – carries risks, but it is fulfilling. Nor is there any reason to suppose the collapse of the earlier situation will recur. It is less likely to if you have learned something from the last time. Anyway, surely the way to look at things is that the happiness and fulfilment you achieve will outweigh the pain if things do go wrong again. Going for gold again gives you the opportunity to escape your unhappiness and dissatisfaction about life. Avoiding it guarantees you will stay unhappy and dissatisfied. Life is tough, be tough and face up to it. You only get one chance, don't waste it!

Feeling guilty
Do you find that your worries prevent you enjoying life? This may be due to the fact that you want to punish yourself by not letting yourself be happy.

Rooted in childhood
This sort of behaviour seems to be rooted in a lack of self worth, originating in childhood. People who suffer in this way often come from homes where they have been mentally and/or physically abused. If a child is abused and punished for nothing, it develops the feeling that it is not fit to be loved or approved of.

The importance of happiness
Some families hold the value that happiness is, in some way, wrong and that life should be viewed as burdensome. This 'original sin' conception invites self punishment. It found its ultimate expression in the flagellators, an ancient religious sect who would publicly whip

themselves in the market place.

A view that the appropriate state of mind is not a happy one is misguided. You only have to consider the nature of pleasure and its place in evolution to realise this. The prime purpose of all species on this earth is to survive and multiply. Whether you prefer to base your conclusions on the scientific (Darwinian) or the religious (Garden of Eden) knowledge, this remains the case. If something is pleasurable and causes happiness, it will be repeated. If it does not, it will not. Therefore, anything which causes pleasure and happiness must be consistent with the primary and natural purpose of life – the survival of the species. Furthermore, we now know from medical and psychological evidence that pleasure and happiness are conducive (and, in fact, important) to good health. Unhappiness, pain and stress are not. It is a fact that people can actually die of a broken heart.

Lastly, so important is pleasure as the driving force for action that those who consistently seek punishment become sadomasochistic. They begin to derive pleasure from punishment they receive, albeit a perverse, or abnormal pleasure.

The message is: strive to be happy. Strive for pleasure. Follow your desire.

Dealing with expectations of others

We are all restricted by other people's expectations of us.

Acting out a role

Social life is a drama unfolding. Everyone is allotted a role and expected to act it out. It is up to them to learn the behaviour that goes with that role. They fail to do so at their peril, for they will be punished by ostracism and ridicule by others present.

The role you are allotted may not be the role you want to play, though. If it is not, the cast may not permit you to take another part. However, you should realise you are free to leave the set and join another play.

Friends and colleagues will resist any demand that they accept any change in your behaviour, or self concept. Everyone likes situations which they have got used to. They know how to respond. Furthermore, if you attempt to upgrade your status, it may arouse envy.

Acting out 'of' role

Nevertheless, you only get one shot at this life – you might as well go for gold, if that's what you want. If you don't, you'll always be disappointed. So be prepared to act **out of role** if necessary. It will be uncomfortable, but liberating. Regardless of the dramaturgical pressures, decide what you want and change your role if necessary. Be consistent, though. Nobody will ever accept someone who keeps changing from one thing to another, or someone who changes and changes back again.

Playing others at their own game

Colleagues at work are another source of restriction on personal growth. This is because of the competitive nature of the workplace. A lot of politics go on at work. People jockey for positions and the stronger personalities will try hard to prevent people on lower levels, or the same level, advancing. Learn the politics and, when necessary, play the game by the same rules.

Dealing with parent problems

Fear of confrontations

Do you fear arguments and confrontations? Some people have a phobia about confrontations, or arguments. When reactions are this strong it is likely that they witnessed a lot of arguments between their parents and these frightened them. They felt guilty, believing the arguments were over them. They grew up feeling a debt must be repaid to their parents.

Children are utterly dependent on their parents in the first few years of life. Consequently, if things are unsettled in the family their very existence is threatened. They are likely to grow up with a sense of ontological insecurity, a fear of the future. They are likely to fear what it will be like when their parents are no longer there. Such children will go to extraordinary lengths to please their parents.

If you recognise this in yourself the time to address it is now. Tell yourself that as a child you wrongly blamed yourself for your parents' arguments. This was because you had no other way of interpreting them. As an infant, the world simply consisted of you and them. You believed it was because of you they were unhappy. These responses stayed with you into adult life. Your task is to overwrite them with more appropriate responses. Tell yourself, you are an adult now. You know this belief is wrong. Start standing up to arguments; they are part of life. Feel the fear and deal with the arguments regardless. The more you do it, the easier it will become.

When you are no longer afraid of arguments you will be more socially successful and assertive.

Dealing with sulking
Sulking is one of the ways highly obstinate people seek to control the lives of others. Sulking is withholding love and affection. Don't give in to it. It reflects an attitude on the part of the sulker that they have an automatic right to something. It may be they feel they have a right to your undivided attention. Tell them, assertively, that this is not the case.

Don't mistake sulking for feelings of rejection or embarrassment on the part of the other person, though. If either of these is the case they should be treated sensitively.

If you have a tendency to sulk, change it. The sulker is never happy sulking and if happiness is your main goal, sulking will get in the way.

Leftovers from strict upbringings

Being afraid of asking
Some children are repeatedly told not to ask for things. Such children find it difficult to ask for things as adults. If you don't ask for things, though, you simply don't get them. You have to overcome this conditioning if you are to succeed in life. Feel the fear of asking, but ask nevertheless. Eventually the fear will decrease.

Write yourself a script telling yourself that:

> People will not know what I want unless I ask. There is nothing wrong with asking. Despite the wrong conditioning I received as a child, I now ask for things I want without hesitation.

Sometimes parents are so strict that they will not let their child ever challenge them. The child's views are never taken into account. Such parents may punish the child by not speaking to them. This is a very harsh punishment, because it is felt as rejection and rejection is hard to bear. These feelings are carried on into adulthood. Here the parent can enforce compliance and control their adult life the way they want them to live. All they have to do is once again, cut them off – cease to speak to them if they do not conform to their wishes.

When energy develops in anything it must go outwards or inwards. If it is pent up it will eventually either explode or implode.

If it explodes it will make waves, which will soon be over. If it implodes it will do damage inside.

This is what happens when a person feels unable to express their feelings. They eventually explode or implode. If the person has been subject to a very strict upbringing, they may have become conditioned to withholding their feelings. Such people will suffer ever increasing damage to their physical and mental health. The former will be in the form of: stomach ulcers, heart disease, strokes, auto-immune deficiencies and skin diseases, such as eczema and psoriasis. The latter will be in the form of depression, anxiety and other neuroses.

Recognising the parent from hell

One of the most limiting conditions of all is the enslaving parent. Some parents, because of neurotic personality and lack of attention from their own partners, control their adult children's lives in a way that secures, for them, all their attention and total compliance with their wishes.

Emotional blackmail

'Look what I've done for you and this is how you repay me?', they might say. Or, more devious still: 'Your poor Daddy is ill and has not long for this earth. You're making him worse by taking the line you are, carrying on with that partner of yours.'

Being neurotic, they are subconsciously aware that they can never be happy themselves. They see their only chance of normalisation being to bring others close to them down to their own level. If nobody is happy that's OK, at least they have someone to share their unhappiness with. If they allow you to be happy, the contrast reminds them how unhappy they themselves are. Furthermore, happiness would liberate the child, who would no longer be dependent upon the parent for relief from unhappiness. Their efforts are often so strong, and so manipulative, that they effectively turn their adult child into a zombie, a shell through which the parent may live their own life.

Attention vampires

The adult child may literally be an attention slave, so that the parent can voraciously feed upon them, drawing every ounce of attention, only to cut them off when their appetite has been satiated, leaving the offspring insecure and frightened until the next time the parent wants to feed. By that time, the offspring is so desperate to obtain acceptance again that they actually crave the parent's hunger for their attention. So the cycle of bloodsucking goes on, the parent milking the very life blood from the offspring, draining any chance of them ever developing an ego of their own. What will such a person do when the parent has passed on from this world? Children of such parents develop mouse-like characteristics, running their lives on the principle of endearment.

What is often the final conclusion of this battle of wills is the offspring's *identification* with the parent's personality. It is well known that people who are highly afraid of another person make themselves grow more and more like that person. The irrational and unconscious motive is that if they achieve the ultimate in copying them they will be that person themselves. You cannot get more like a person than the person themself. The irrational assumption is that that person would not be able to hurt themself. There is evidence that some Jews in the Nazi concentration camps wore swastikas on their arms for this reason.

Consequently, their own individual personality becomes repressed and they exhibit the personality of their oppressor. At first, such a person might switch between manifestations of their own, real self and the personality of their parent. Eventually, however, the parent personality will dominate. The old, real personality will become so submerged that it will, for all intents and purposes, be lost forever.

Always someone else's fault
Neurotic parents often look for scapegoats, too. They blame others for everything. They project their guilt away from themselves. Some of it will be projected onto their partner, if still living. Sometimes the child gets the burden. If the latter is grown up, it may be *their* partner who is targeted. Nobody will escape entirely, for nothing is ever the parent's fault: it is always someone else's.

If a grown up son or daughter of a neurotic and enslaving parent in the end identifies with that parent, i.e. internalises that parent's personality, they will inherit all that parent's traits. The imposing and dominating personality of their enslaving parent will have effectively killed off their own.

Breaking free
If you recognise this state, the time to act is now. If you are a child of an attention vampire break free before it is too late. That is not to say you should stop loving that parent, but you must assertively redirect their efforts. You should address the problem boldly, face to face.

We are a pair-bonding species and one day every little pig grows up and builds their own house of straw. It's the natural way. To allow a parent to prevent you doing this for their own selfish reasons is unacceptable. That parent will not be there one day and you'll be too old to make a relationship to fill the gap.

Tell them they are draining you of your attention when you need to direct some of it to your partner. Tell them you are grown up now. Tell them that the proper person who should be giving them the daily attention they need is their own partner (your father, or mother, as the case may be). If that person is deceased then tell your widowed parent that they must make efforts to find a new partner or new friends to serve their attention needs. Tell your parent that they are sucking you dry and whilst you will always love them they must step aside and let you get on with your life. Tell them that if they won't, then you will cut them off. Use the same threat as they have been successfully using on you. It will work, because they are afraid of losing your attention.

Worry is futile and wasteful

Do you worry about things – exams, work, bills, etc? Do you feel guilty about things you've done or not done? Do you find yourself preoccupied with regrets? Does the worrying help? Does it relieve the feelings at all? No, of course it doesn't.

Worrying about something does not improve the situation; it just makes you less able to cope with it.

There is an old Tibetan saying that if a problem is resolvable then there is no point in worrying about it, because it can be resolved. If it is not resolvable, there is no point in worrying about it, because it won't help.

Worrying often creates self-fulfilling prophecies

The truth goes even further than that, though. Worrying about something makes it into a self-fulfilling prophecy. If you are worried about being unable to deal with something difficult, the act of worrying will wear you down and fill your head with negative thoughts. It will make you doubt your ability to do what you have to do. All these things will affect your strength of will. They will also affect your concentration and other mental powers, your physical ability, your stress level and your expectations of success. By worrying about something you have to do, you increase the likelihood that you will fail to do it.

Filling your head with positive thoughts
Suppose you have a lecture to give. Suppose you are worried that you will forget your lines, or that you will blush or stammer. Fill your head, instead, with positive thoughts and images. See yourself succeeding. Feel the pride. Interrupt any negative thoughts creeping in and replace them with positive ones.

Remember that your subconscious mind cannot distinguish the real from the imagined. Therefore, if you imagine success your subconscious mind will record the feelings which go with it – confidence, pride, competence, etc. These will be played back when the time comes to do it for real.

The unlikelihood of insolubility
There is always a way to solve a problem. If there were insoluble ones, don't you think you would have encountered them before?

Dealing with stress
Do you suffer from stress? Do you find it difficult to switch off after work? Are you irritable and tearful? Do you snap at people? Do you feel you cannot cope with the tasks in front of you? Are you a workaholic? Is your sex life unsatisfactory? Do you suffer from stomach ulcers?

Stress is the mental and physical response to a situation seen as impossible. Examples of sources of stress include:

- a workload seen as impossible

- a job seen as unmanageable

- a relationship seen as intolerable

- debts which you feel cannot possibly be repaid

- a financial crisis which, it appears, cannot be resolved

- an important appointment which you are going to miss due to travel delays.

Stress gets the body ready for fight or flight. However, in today's world that response will not achieve the result we need. Only rational, problem solving thought will enable us to deal with the demands of modern living. Stress suppresses our ability in this respect. Consequently, to master your life you need to master stress.

Knowing the consequences of prolonged stress
If stress occurs over a long period, physical illness will result. If this happens you will lose some control over your life and destiny. Symptoms of stress to watch out for are as follows:

- aggressiveness
- tearfulness
- feelings of frustration
- absent-mindedness
- indecisiveness
- low self-esteem
- anxiety
- depression
- poor concentration
- headaches and neck aches
- nail biting or skin biting habits
- perspiring
- palpitations
- dizziness
- feelings of nausea
- loss of appetite
- insomnia
- increased drinking
- chain smoking
- sexual difficulties

Dealing with acute stress attacks
If you feel an acute attack of stress, remove yourself from the environment in which the feeling of stress began. Do some deep breathing exercises (see page 77). Only when you feel calm should you go back into the situation and address the problem.

Some things you can do to reduce your stress level
- Ask yourself: Are the tasks you see as impossible really impossible? If you answer yes, then renegotiate your acceptance of the responsibility to carry them out.

- Stop trying to do several things at once.

- Plan what you are going to do.

- Be realistic.

- Stop promising to meet impossible deadlines. Be assertive to those who try to make you accept more than you can handle.

- Consider which of your tasks can be delegated.

Make the best use of the morning. In most cases energy levels are highest during this time. Note down anything left to do at the end of each day, so that you do not take things home on your mind.

Finding relief from stress
If you find it difficult to switch off after work perhaps it's time for a holiday. It's no good just having a week off work, you will still be surrounded by your files and reminders of what you have to do. Moreover, you will be in a position to do things about them. You need to get right away, where you have no reminders and no means of tinkering with your problems – a complete break.

Some people deal with stress by having a hobby or a pastime. This requires them to switch off from their everyday concerns. A new environment, different clothes, different people all have the effect of helping us to break away from things that are getting us down.

Internal states have external counterparts (see page 43). You can reduce your stress level by manipulating your posture and other aspects of your physiology. Adjust your body parts so they represent the outward signs of relaxation and the mental state will, to some degree, follow suit. Unlock your clenched fingers, unclench your jaws, sit back, unhunch your shoulders, smile, breathe deeply, slowly and evenly.

Some people find words of self-reassurance help. Try writing yourself a script, saying something like this:

> I do my best in all circumstances, but I do not, and will not, expect any more of myself than that. I recognise my limitations. I do one thing at a time and do not let anyone hassle me to do

otherwise. I keep myself calm and relaxed with all the outward signs of relaxation and refuse to let people hassle me. When I leave work, I switch off from it.

If problems seem insoluble, think to yourself:

...but somehow I've got over every obstacle that has presented itself to me so far. Why should I feel it will be any different from here on? It just sometimes looks as if it will be.

Analysing the problem
It may look as though there is no solution to a problem, but our perception is limited. We can't see everything at once. Furthermore, we make assumptions about things and we try to work within them. Invariably, though, they can be changed and the problem becomes soluble.

Instead of reacting to a problem, analyse it. Stand back and look to see whether any of the assumptions can be changed. That is what problem solving is at the end of the day – a task that is impossible on the present assumptions.

Stress and your sex life

Stress affects your sex life and, conversely, a poor sex life affects your well-being and concept of self-worth. The role of stress is to get the body ready to face danger. The reproductive urge is the last thing needed in such a situation. You will feel stress in tense back, neck and shoulder muscles. A massage by your partner will help ease the muscular tension, but you also have to let go of the problems on your mind. To feel sexy you have to have images in your head. Stress prevents this.

Good sex just happens; it's not a question of effort or will. If stress is causing sex to be poor, then worrying it about it won't help. It will just cause feelings of inadequacy. This will increase the stress, making it even less likely.

Overcoming insomnia

Do you find problems keep you awake at night? Do you lie and worry about things? You will never see them realistically at such time. You will focus on the negative aspects. This is because your circadian rhythm is at its lowest point in the early hours of the morning and you are more prone to negative thoughts.

The trouble is when the body is least active the mind is most active. If you cannot switch off, then get up and make a drink, read, or do something else. Don't just lie and fret. You will just wear yourself out and make yourself less able to cope successfully with the thing that is worrying you.

If you regularly have trouble sleeping, avoid drinking tea or coffee before going to bed. Wind down well before turning in. Things which will help you do this include: listening to music, reading, or going for a walk.

Inducing sleep

When you have nothing to do and your imagination is still you are in a state of boredom. Animals fall asleep when they have nothing to do – when they are bored. It once occurred to me that to guarantee sleep all you had to do was induce total boredom, by complete thought-stopping. So I, concentrated on keeping any thoughts at all from crossing my mind. It was a sort of negative meditation, rather than concentrating on something, I concentrated on 'nothing' and on keeping a state of 'nothingness' before my mind's eye.

Before long I had an experience which I can only describe as like falling down a hole into sleep. It was scary because of the loss of control that it implied and I quickly forced myself out of it.

I did not try it again until I had a migraine one day. When you are suffering from an acute migraine attack, you really don't care what happens to you as long as you are out of it. I tried this technique again then and the same thing happened. I felt I was falling down a hole into sleep. This time, however, I let myself go. When I awoke my migraine was gone. I had slept for five hours.

Since then, I have used this technique often. It sends you rapidly into sleep and once you have overcome the fear of the sudden descent, you become prepared to use it whenever necessary.

If this does not work for you, another technique is to try to make yourself stay awake. Think how many times you've tried to keep your eyes open to watch a film or read a book. In the end, you've succumbed to sleep. Kid your body into this state.

Relaxating by breathing

Sit with crossed legs, hands on knees, palms outwards, forefinger and thumb together. This is almost the lotus position. Some find the complete position difficult, so this will do. It is good for relaxation.

Breathe in from the stomach. Place your hand on your stomach and feel it expand. Hold the breath for a count of roughly five seconds and then exhale, contracting your stomach as you do. Repeat nine times.

Just concentrate on what you are doing, nothing else. If other things intrude (and they will) don't forcibly block them out, because that will make you tense. Instead, just let them float by, as if you are watching them pass by on a conveyor belt. They will probably cause you no tension just by being there. It is only if you engage with them that tension will occur. Don't try to stop them appearing in front of your eyes, but don't let them significantly affect your thinking. Stare straight through them as if they are not there.

Don't be afraid of mistakes

See mistakes in a positive way. Use them as resources to make sure you get it right next time. Nobody can ever learn anything without making a mistake, they can only internalise knowledge. You only learn when you discover what happens if you do it wrong. This is one of the main reasons why young people won't learn from the errors of their parents. They have got to make their own mistakes.

YOUR TEN-POINT PLAN OF ACTION

1. Take responsibility for your life.

2. Take stock of the present.

3. List the changes you desire.

4. Break down your goals.

5. Set targets.

6. Make preparations.

7. Banish negative thoughts.

8. Start each day with a positive thinking ritual in front of a mirror.

9. Fill your mind with positive images of the achieved goal.

10. Throughout each day, hold the crown of your head high and believe yourself capable of great things.

Start right away. Don't postpone it.

SUMMARY

- There are ways to develop confidence.

- There are ways to overcome loneliness.

- Learn to love yourself.

- Don't be a mouse.

- Don't be Mr Nice Guy, who is everyone's shoulder to cry on, but nobody's lover.

- You can transcend the expectations of others.

- Don't be afraid of success.

- Banish unwarranted feelings of guilt.

- Face up to fear of arguments.

- Don't bottle up your feelings.

- Learn to ask for what you want.

- Stand up to problem parents.

- Worrying does no good.

- Deal with stress.

- Strive to be happy.

DISCUSSION POINTS

1. How socially confident are you on a rising scale of 1 to 5?

2. Do you ever feel lonely and, if so, how often?

3. Do you bottle up your feelings?

4. Prior to reading this book, how much scope for change did you feel you had?

6
Using Your Conscious Mind

The next chapter deals with sharpening up the effectiveness of your conscious mind. If your subconscious mind has not been liberated from its hang-ups, all the cerebral skills and qualities in the world will not bring you success. Conversely, however, you may have a highly liberated subconscious, but if you don't have well developed thinking and learning skills, any high ambitions you have in life will remain out of reach.

DEVELOPING YOUR THINKING SKILLS

There are various activities in thinking. Here are some examples:

- focusing
- asking the right questions
- defining areas of attention
- analysis
- synthesis
- abstraction.

Focusing
To think effectively you need to develop the ability to focus on a specific range of detail. Our **perceptual set** enables us to handle only a limited amount of detail. Therefore, if you do not develop your ability to focus selectively you will find that you will not be able to comprehend or solve multi-faceted problems. It is sometimes because we cannot see all of the elements of a problem together that it appears insoluble. If we could, the answer might be simple. The more you teach yourself to focus selectively, the more of the relevant details you will be able to focus upon.

Asking the right questions

Often the reason a problem appears unmanageable, or even unapproachable, is because you have not formulated any relevant questions to ask. Formulating the right questions is one of the keys to effectively solving problems.

Analysing

The ability to analyse is crucial to developing understanding. Analysis involves splitting things up into elements and then looking for ways of classifying them. Suppose, for example, you were planning how to secure electoral support from your local community in a local authority election. It would be important to try to understand the nature of the electorate. Relevant classifications you would make would be things like socio-economic group, level of income, area of residence, occupation, nationality, sex, age, marital status, whether they have children and so on. Your analysis would tell you what proportion of your electorate came under each heading.

Synthesising

Synthesis is drawing together the separated elements in an analysis to form a different, meaningful whole to that from which you started. Using the same example, the analysed data would be used to construct a single picture of the electorate in terms of its characteristics. It might reveal that your electorate is more or less equal in terms of the sexes, predominantly homeowners in the higher income bracket, mostly aged between 25 and 50 and mostly skilled white collar workers or above. From this you could effectively define your manifesto.

Abstracting

Abstracting means extracting the general principles involved in a number of situations. Suppose it was apparent to an economic observer that retail sales figures were higher than they had been for a number of years. Houses were starting to sell more quickly and people were purchasing goods on credit more than they had been doing for some time. Conversely, building society deposits were decreasing; people appeared to be spending their money rather than saving it. What would appear common to all of these observations is that people seemed more confident about being able to afford things, being able to replenish savings and pay back their borrowings on their credit cards than had seemed to be the case for some time. Such an economic observer would say a 'feel good factor' appeared to be present. This is the abstraction.

Using abstract terms
One of the practices which will help you make abstractions is to use abstract terms. This means instead of being specific, be as general as you can. Rather than saying people appear more prepared to borrow money, spend money and use up what they have saved for a rainy day, choose more abstract terminology and say their spending behaviour seems more optimistic than it has been for some time.

Another aspect of abstraction is choosing the level at which to abstract. The higher the level the greater the abstraction. Take a motor car engine as an example. A low level of abstraction will explain its workings in terms of an exothermic chemical reaction from the combustion of petrol and oxygen. At a higher level of analysis it will be explained in terms of a machine which does work and which is powered by the products of combustion. At an even higher level of analysis it is a motor car.

ACQUIRING KNOWLEDGE AND MENTAL SKILLS

Breaking through the plateau
Have you noticed how learning tends to plateau? You get so far and then your progress sticks. It is not necessarily that your desire and determination have dried up, it is more likely that the methods you used to reach your present level are not appropriate for surpassing it. New techniques must be devised, and you have to find them.

Start experimenting again to find a technique which will bring you further. Here are some suggestions to help you find a way forward:

- try planning and preparing in great detail
- try without any preparation at all
- work intensively for a period
- work in a casual way for a period
- vary your speeds of work
- work at different times of the day.

The principle of persistent hesitation
Our knowledge gels into rigid structures if we let it. We only

continue to learn whilst those structures retain some flexibility. To prolong our ability to learn, whether we are talking about a particular subject or about 'learnability' in life generally, we must resist early fixations of ideas.

Always look for different solutions, using the whole range of your experience. Interact with your knowledge by looking for possible objections. Use these as starting points for further exploration, designing defences to your view, or looking for other solutions which these objections suggest. You should aim for not only extensive knowledge, but also fine tuning of operation in using it. When you feel you have gained a mastery of something, test your proficiency on others. Discuss the knowledge you've learned, welcome criticism, although you should distinguish the constructive from the destructive kinds and ignore the latter. Constructive criticism will contain defensible argument, destructive criticism will not.

Discouragement is always in plentiful supply. It is a common social trait. If one member of a group aspires to greater achievement than the others, the group will discourage him. 'Don't be daft, you can't do that', they will say. This is because a shared world view and a common achievement level is important for the group members' emotional security. If anyone rocks the boat it shows up the inadequacy of the rest.

Adjusting the pressure

- Make your early learning endeavours as easy and anxiety free as you can.

- Don't be too concerned about speed.

- Don't be too preoccupied with avoiding errors.

- Whatever you do don't try to master great chunks of the subject all at once.

- Take nibbles, not bites.

- In the early stages, do not plan your learning in terms of set periods of study, but, rather, in terms of the achievement of 'learning objectives'.

Seeking out general principles

General principles remain constant, but applications vary. Only when you have looked at many different applications can you really say you have a grasp of the general principle.

- Relate your learning to your interests.

- Aim to develop as wide an experience in your chosen field as possible.

- Formulate your arguments in different styles.

- Reformulate them to apply them to imaginary problems.

Consolidating your gains

Tell people what you've learned. Discuss it with them at length. All their responses, verbal and non-verbal, and everything you do to help them understand the message will become associated in your memory with the material you have learned. This will consolidate your learning and make it easier for you to recall. The more people you talk to about it the better your consolidation and recall potential will be.

Real understanding and learning

You cannot say you really understand an argument until you've considered all its strengths and weaknesses. You can only say you've learnt a piece of knowledge when you've related it to other knowledge.

Getting more knowledge with less effort

Learning doesn't simply mean increasing your knowledge. It means finding ways of doing the same, but with less effort. Here you have an important secret of motivation. Approach learning in this way and you will have turned what de-motivates most people (the prospect of all that effort) into a motivator (the prospect of less of all that effort). Research shows that the highest achievers actually spend less time on study than those who achieve at more modest levels.

Learning how to learn

How often is it said that if you want to achieve something enough you will achieve it. It isn't true. To achieve something you have to **will** it, too.

What's the difference between wishing and willing something? A *wish* is passive, like putting your tooth under the pillow. *Willing* is active. In today's world you've got to *make* things happen. To learn something you have to develop a **will to learn**. This involves analysing what you've got going for you and what your weaknesses are. Devoting yourself to a serious quest for ways of improving your learning is not the same thing as ways of increasing your knowledge.

You have to **learn to learn**. Many highly intelligent people never do this, because in their early years of education they got by with intuition, whereas most had to develop skills. Later on, when those skills are necessary, when their intuition won't suffice for the more complex problems, the highly intelligent ones very often lose out: they've never 'learned how to learn'. Consequently, they become alienated at school, blame the curriculum, say it's too slow for them and settle into a life of low achievement.

Practice doesn't necessarily make perfect

The old saying that 'practice makes perfect' is misleading, In fact, a too ready reliance on practice is more likely to ensure imperfection. Let us see why.

Repetition is not the best way of learning, for it can lead to **practice error**. Does continuous walking make someone a more skilled walker? Does repeated driving make someone a better driver? Think about it! No, it usually makes them a worse one. Does increased handwriting make someone a better handwriter? Those who write most often tend to have the worst handwriting.

We all tend to make more errors and ineffective actions than accurate and effective actions. If we learned by repetition we would all deteriorate in all of our abilities.

Furthermore, if repetition were the source of learning, then we would only be able to apply our learning to identical sets of circumstances to those in which we practised.

In the early stages of learning something, we err more than we succeed, yet it is in this phase that most learning takes place. It can't be the repetition that's teaching us.

Don't practise – experiment

Always vary your procedures. You can then discover which is best. Find different approaches. Do more thinking than acting. Analyse what you are going to do before you do it and afterwards review it. Your goals should be not simply to achieve an error-free result, but to become familiar with the conditions and behaviour which bring it about. You are educating your will to learn, making it a more and more formidable force. Learn to recognise success, how you achieved it and what it feels like.

USING YOUR MEMORY

According to the two-process theory of memory there are separate long and short-term processes involved. Short-term memory is enhanced by **chunking**. Long-term memory works by **association**.

There is a competing theory in which there are not two separate parts, but merely one. Whether material is retained over time depends on how deeply it is processed. What has been said about chunking and association would still apply, however. Chunking would still enhance what goes in and association would still determine what stays there, for chunking works at the perceptual level while association works at the storage level.

I will not go into great detail on memory enhancement strategies here, for readers can obtain this information in my other book *Maximising Your Memory*, in this series. Instead, I will just provide a basic explanation of what chunking and association are and how we can use them to make the best of our memory capabilities. *Maximising Your Memory* contains strategies specifically designed for each kind of memory task.

Chunking

Chunking is grouping items into meaningful categories. It may be hard for us to remember a shopping list containing:

- bread
- eggs
- butter
- bacon
- toilet soap
- shampoo
- tomatoes
- coffee
- cornflakes
- washing powder
- tea
- lettuce
- cucumber
- radishes
- washing-up liquid.

However, it would be reasonably easy to remember:

- breakfast foods
- beverages
- salad ingredients

- household cleaning items
- toiletries.

Nor will it be difficult for us to remember that the breakfast foods contained cornflakes, bacon, bread, butter, eggs, tomatoes, the beverage list contained tea and coffee, the salad ingredients contained lettuce, cucumber and radishes, the household cleaning group contained washing powder and washing-up liquid and the toiletries group contained toilet soap and shampoo.

The message is to chunk it carefully before you begin to store material in your head. If you can use a mnemonic to help you remember the items in each group, then better still. To give you an example, you could remember the six items in the breakfast foods category, i.e., bacon, bread, cornflakes, eggs, butter and tomatoes by making a memorable catchphrase using words that have the same initial letters as the items in the list. Such a catchphrase might be: busy breakfast cooks eat burnt toast.

Associating
If you want to store material over a long period of time, then the trick is to associate it with something. It could be a rhyme. For example, if you want to remember the name John Wright, think John Wright gives you a fright and imagine him being a bit grotesque in appearance.

Alternatively, you could associate a name with a quality, or attribute of the person. For example, if you wish to remember the name Frances Gardener, you might visualise her in her garden.

Combining the two
Sometimes it is easy to combine the two – attribute and rhyme. An example might be a tall lady called Elizabeth Jones. Say to yourself 'Elizabeth Jones has long bones'.

Of course, a natural way of associating material is to think about it, because in so doing you are comparing it with material you already have in your head. You are thus associating it in a very meaningful way and so it is not surprising that the more you think about something the more you will remember it.

PROBLEM SOLVING

A problem often amounts to the need to overcome an obstacle in the path to some goal. Alternatively, it can be that you simply have unsufficient information to enable you to proceed.

Moving in and moving out

There are three basic approaches you can take to problem solving:

- moving in
- moving out
- combining the two.

Moving in

Moving in is when you know what you want to achieve and you have to work out how to arrive at it. It involves planning your resources and methods and working out how to get round any obstacles in the way.

This type of problem is simply something we cannot solve on the present assumptions. We have to decide which assumptions can be changed.

The stages of problem solving, where a *moving in* approach is used are as follows:

- define the problem

- assess your resources

- model the process

- solve the problem.

Moving out

Moving out is where you know the starting point, but not the end point. An example might be where you have a sum of money to invest, but you don't know where to invest it. Another example might be where a person is trying to decide what university courses to apply for, or what career path they should take.

Moving out and then moving in

Sometimes we only know the type of goal we seek, rather than the specific goal. An example might be where a company is looking for a way of using its spare factory capacity. The general goal may be to find a proposition which will be profitable, will use all the spare capacity and require no further significant investment. Various ideas will be generated using the nature of the spare capacity as the starting point. When a range of proposals have been drafted they will then each be considered in terms of their relative merit in achieving the goal of the best and most profitable utilisation of the spare capacity.

Brainstorming, followed by reverse brainstorming, is an example of this process of *moving out and then moving in*. Brainstorming is where a group of people, ideally no more than six, generate ideas from a fixed starting point, using free association. The important thing is that in this stage of the process there should be no evaluation of the ideas, just generation of them. Following this, the ideas generated are evaluated in terms of a set of criteria. At this stage there is no generation of ideas, just evaluation.

Making decisions
A distinction is sometimes made between decision making and decision taking. **Decision making** is selecting a range of alternative courses of action in pursuit of a specific goal. **Decision taking** is choosing between these alternatives. Decision taking always involves some degree of chance and the decision taker will assess which alternative provides the best risk/benefit quotient. The more information you have the less decision taking responsibility is involved. If you have complete information there will be no decision to take, as there will only be one course of action which provides the best risk/benefit quotient. In decision behaviour the goal should always be to generate as much information as possible, within the constraints of time and money, and after taking into consideration other demands on your attention and resources.

Using stock solutions
Two general ways of solving problems are:

- working backwards
- going around the obstacle.

Other considerations
You also need to consider the following:

- whether you have a good solution, but to the wrong problem

- whether the answer is consistent with your grand plan

- whether your answer to the problem is workable

- whether your solution to the problem will create other problems.

Working backwards
Have you noticed when you call out the AA, the RAC, or any other roadside repair service, they tend to trace the course of the problem backwards? If your engine is not firing, they will first check your spark plugs are sparking. If they are not, then they will trace it back to where the spark plugs' current comes from, i.e., the distributor, and so on. All problems of malfunctioning can be treated in this fault-finding way.

When we focus on a particular problem, our thinking tends to become rather rigid and we block out things which are not directly connected with it. This is very useful and, indeed, it's a skill you can, and should, enhance. It is known as **focusing**. However, it is also useful to be able to release this rigidity of thinking when you feel it is necessary.

By releasing your rigidity of thinking you open up the possibility of finding indirect routes to your goal. You may also see other opportunities which you may wish to pursue if the present one is, in the end, found to be unfeasible.

The skill of switching from rigidly focusing upon one set of concerns to a wider focus upon unconnected concepts is known as **lateral thinking** – stepping sideways.

THINKING CREATIVELY

Some people find it difficult to be creative in their thinking. They prefer, and have been taught, to follow fixed paths. There are various ways, however, in which you can develop your ability to think creatively. One such way is to change the sub-modalities of ideas you have in mind (for the meaning of sub-modalities see page 40). For example, if you wish to gain the optimum benefit from the limited amount of capital you have and you are considering buying a house and a car, you could consider each in terms of age and size.

Avoiding fanciful ideas
Being creative and being fanciful are different things. Being creative is seeking sensible ideas which are consistent with a goal and represent feasible pursuits. Fanciful ideas, in contrast, are merely daydreaming and include what you would like to have, or to be, regardless of whether it is really within reach. One way of avoiding fanciful ideas is to have definite starting points. Some examples of these are:

- a list of present assets

- a list of personal qualities

- a list of opportunities you have missed, but would have liked to have taken up

- synergistic possibilities: these are separate plans leading to separate goals which may be in some way complementary, each adding to the other's potential

- variable value opportunities: these are where you can find an opportunity from something someone else discards

- a list of your needs

- a list of weaknesses in your present system of operating

- a list of improvements you feel you could feasibly make to the quality of your life, or your career

- a list of achievements you have admired in others and would like to emulate

- current trends in lifestyle which you have not yet managed to latch on to but would like to

- list of weaknesses you would like to turn into strengths.

Thinking to order
You should be aware that when you are seeking something that fits with planned requirements you may, by focusing rigidly, overlook an alternative which might give you even greater utility.

Provocation
Ideas can be generated by experiments to see where a particular line of thinking will lead. Begin your questioning with: 'What if...'

Using fictitious problems
Another way of generating ideas is to create a fictitious problem and try to solve it. Afterwards, consider whether any of the ideas you have generated will help you either directly or indirectly in a real problem you have to solve. What I mean by indirectly is: do any of the ideas spark off other ideas which will help? This amounts to stepping sideways and is, therefore, a kind of lateral thinking.

Brainstorming
Brainstorming is also a useful way of generating ideas. It has been

explained on page 89 in the section dealing with problem solving.

Looking for opportunities
Train yourself to always be on the lookout for opportunities. You have to search for them, or at least spot them as they float past, they will rarely come to you.

Expanding your knowledge base
Ideas come from other ideas. It is always, therefore, a good idea to expand your knowledge base. Read widely, both fiction and non-fiction. Keep up to date with current affairs, by reading quality newspapers. Teach yourself to understand the stock market, the arts and what is going on the world.

ACQUIRING PHYSICAL SKILLS

When you are trying to learn a physical skill you have two goals, *a successful result* and *the means to it*. You should concentrate on the means to it, rather than the result itself. The reason for this is that your earliest attempts are likely to be the most ineffective. The failure data is stored in your subconscious and will be relived when you try again. This is the opposite of what you want.

Focusing on the means
Instead, focus on the means to the result you want. Break the process down into sub-goals, as appropriate and practise those until you get them right. Sub-goals are, obviously, easier to attain. You are, therefore, more likely to store success data in your subconscious than if you were focusing on the overall goal.

Examine the processes for achieving your sub-goals very carefully. Watch an expert performing them and try to imagine what they feel like as they do. Each time you get a less than perfect result, analyse exactly why it was the case and do it differently next time. Keep changing your performance until you get it right.

You can overdo the segmentation of the process, however. There will be parts of the process which you can achieve quite adequately from the start. There is no point in breaking such sub-processes down any further. You should break the processes down purposefully. Try for the overall result first and then assess exactly where your weaknesses in the process seem to be.

As an example, suppose you were learning to play the guitar. You would probably begin by learning about three chords, say C, F and

G7. You would then take a song simple enough to require only these three chords for an accompaniment. The traditional song *The Foggy, Foggy Dew* is an example. Try singing along with the song and changing chords where necessary. You would soon find you had little difficulty changing between G7 and C, but that changing from C to F was hard for a beginner. Consequently, you would have discovered a sub-skill to segment from the rest – changing from C to F. When you have mastered this, so that you can make the change smoothly and almost without thinking, try accompanying the full song again.

Storing more positive data
If you identify sub-goals that you need to work for before achieving the overall goal, you will store more positive data. The more positive data you store, the more positive will be your experience, as you work towards your overall goal. The more positive your experience the more motivated you will be.

One way to help you learn sub-tasks involved in a complex skill is to do other things which involve those sub-skills. Footballers, for example, could benefit by learning various kinds of dancing, e.g. tap. Golfers could benefit by playing tennis and tennis players by playing squash and badminton. Aspiring pianists would benefit from taking up typing and vice versa. Boxers might take up disco dancing and runners could gain by taking up long jump and hurdles.

Developing social skills
It is the same with social skills. Set small goals and scrutinise them finely, then vary your approach until you get them just right.

Distinguishing strength from skill
Some people focus most of their effort on 'going the distance'. Newcomers to typing often concentrate on getting a certain amount of pages done in a certain amount of time, rather than improving their skill in moving between different letters on the keyboard. Misguided runners might concentrate their efforts on increasing their distance, rather than on getting their pacing and breathing techniques right. They appear to assume that technique will take care of itself. This can be a mistake. As I have already pointed out, if errors are not corrected as and when they occur, then they are learnt along with the rest of the skill. Technique will not take care of itself. It is far better to split up the process in terms of sub-goals, these being parts of the process currently prone to error. Such errors are then less likely to be learnt and reinforced.

There are other reasons why seeking to 'go the distance' at the expense of accuracy is an error. Such approach, if used in learning to type, can result in repetitive strain injury. If this happens you will have made your goal unattainable for a considerable period to come. Similarly, focusing on 'going the distance' in running at the expense of skill can lead to ligament injury, as you put demands on muscles before they are ready to take them.

Controlling your body

To effectively perform a skill you have to organise the action of those parts of the body which are to move within the postural framework of those parts which are to remain still. The first task is to identify which parts stay still and which parts move. Do this by observing experts.

Relaxing tensions

Tensions in uninvolved parts of the body will cause them to fidget or tremble. This is inconsistent with the sub-goal of keeping the uninvolved postural framework still while the involved parts move. You need to learn to relax tensions in the uninvolved parts of the body.

Breathing

Even the normal process of breathing will cause uninvolved parts of the body to move. Therefore, when a really precise movement has to be achieved, for example, cueing a snooker ball, firing a gun, an arrow, or a dart, hold your breath at the moment of action.

Eye focus

All ball game players are taught to keep their eye on the ball at all times. This is not only because they need to see where it is. Another reason is that we are continuously being bombarded by extrinsic information. Players in a badminton match can easily become distracted by the movements of spectators. Keeping your eye rigidly on the ball is a way of guarding against paying attention to irrelevant data.

Evaluating progress

It is important that you frequently analyse the development of any skill you are trying to master. Constructively criticise different aspects of your performance with a view to improving them.

Making use of real situations

It is always best to practise in real situations. That way skills, sub-skills and success data stored in your subconscious will become associated with the surroundings in which you wish to perform the skills.

Accepting our uniqueness

One last point must be made on this subject. That is that everyone is unique. We all start learning a skill from different starting points. The schemata (mental knowledge maps) and skill foundations we have developed throughout our lives will differ from person to person. So, too, will our physical qualities and our strengths and weaknesses. Consequently, what has been said here about learning physical skills is only a guide. The principles given must be adapted to personal needs.

SUMMARY

- Thinking involves various individual skills.

- There are ways you can greatly enhance your ability to acquire knowledge.

- Your ability to remember things can be enhanced many-fold by learning memory techniques.

- You can become a much more effective problem solver if you learn the relevant techniques.

- There are many ways in which you can improve your creativity.

- You can learn physical skills more efficiently if you use the special techniques.

DISCUSSION POINTS

1. How advanced are your thinking skills?

2. How good is your memory?

3. How good are your problem solving skills?

4. How creative are you?

Appendix
Errors of Mental Storage

DENIAL

Denial is when a person consciously refuses to accept a truth which their psyche cannot handle.

DISPLACEMENT

Displacement refers to an inability to express a negative reaction, such as hate, onto its proper target. It may be because that target is someone close to you. The negative feelings are, instead, shifted onto a person who does not deserve them.

IDENTIFICATION

Identification refers to developing one's personality towards an ever-increasing similarity with an aggressor. An example of the latter might be an overly strict and forceful parent. The motive is an irrational feeling that the more like the aggressor you become the less they will be able to hurt you. If you could achieve the ultimate and become them in every detail, they would not be likely to hurt you. You would, after all, *be them*; they would not do anything which would hurt themselves. While you cannot achieve quite this level of identification, the closer you get the more of this kind of benefit you might obtain.

RATIONALISATION

Rationalisation occurs when a person finds dubious explanations and justifications for behaviour which they cannot really justify to themselves.

REACTION FORMATION

Reaction formation is the development of an extreme aversion or reaction to something in order to defend oneself against the possibility that one's attitude, or feelings towards it, are positive. For example, a latent homosexual may develop an extreme negative reaction to homosexuals to avoid facing the truth about him/herself.

REPRESSION

Repression occurs when someone buries an upsetting memory out of reach, so that they do not even know it is there.

REVERSAL

Reversal refers to turning one's negative feelings towards another person back upon oneself.

SCAPEGOATING

Scapegoating refers to transferring guilty feelings onto another.

Glossary

Adapted child. Part of the psyche consisting of stored strategies you used as a child for gaining positive reactions from others, particularly parents and authority figures.

Analysis. Splitting things up into elements and then looking for ways of classifying them.

Anchors. Things which can secure for you a particular state of mind. There are three main categories of these: *role models, physiology* and *thinking of a time when you were in a desired state*.

Brainstorming. Brainstorming is where a group of people, ideally no more than six, generate ideas from a fixed starting point, using free association. The important thing is that in this stage of the process there should be no evaluation of the ideas, just the generation of them. Following this, the ideas generated are evaluated in terms of a set of criteria. At this stage there is no generation of ideas, just evaluation.

Chunking. Chunking is grouping items into meaningful categories.

Comfort zone. All those situations in which we can operate according to, or close to, our self image. Our minds tell us we are out of our depth, or *slumming it*, and make us feel uncomfortable if the situation we are in is inconsistent with our self image.

Congruence signal. A feature common to all your most effective states of mind.

Constructive motivation. Motivation derived from analysing what we want and why we want it.

Contamination. Although only one of the three parts of the psyche can be dominant at any one time, other parts can interfere with its function to some degree. We call this contamination. The child, or the parent can, for example, impinge upon the functioning of the adult. This will make it less rational, reasonable, or open-minded than it ought to be. When unfounded child, or parent data is accepted as true, the adult part of the psyche rationalises it and justifies it in whatever way it can.

Critical parent. Part of the psyche consisting of stored admonishments and criticism from parents and authority figures during childhood.

Deleting. Noticing and responding to certain aspects and details, but not all. We do not need to attend to everything in a situation if we can get a pretty good idea of its meaning by attending to just a few. We *delete* things to avoid *channel overload* and to enable us to take the material in quickly.

Dissociated states. States of mind which involve a kind of mental disengagement. Only part of the psyche is experiencing them and the full quality of the experience, in all its facets, is not felt.

Distortion. We furnish our inner world by distorting what comes in through our senses. We do it to make it fit more closely with images we have stored in our heads. We then distort our stored images, themselves, to complete the final fit.

Generalisation. Thinking that because other situations, or things, or people of this type have these, or those qualities, this one will too. We tend to generalise about facts, so that we don't have to think too much. It is a shortcut to understanding, but it is not always reliable.

Incongruence signal. A feature common to all your worst states of mind.

Internal dialogues. Situations where two parts of the psyche are disagreeing. First we think we should do something, then we think we shouldn't and then we think we should again. Sometimes it refers to an alternation between self-blame and self-excuse.

Lateral thinking. Switching from rigidly focusing upon one set of concerns to a wider focus upon unconnected concepts and then back again, in order to solve a problem.

Metacognition. Thinking about thinking.

Modalities. Modalities are the essential building blocks of experience. Sub-modalities are the qualities they possess.

Moving in. A term used for a problem-solving approach where you know what you want to achieve and you have to work out how to arrive at it.

Moving out. A term used for a problem-solving approach where you know the starting point, but not the end point. An example might be where you have a sum of money to invest, but you don't known where to invest it. Another example might be where a person is trying to decide what university courses to apply for, or what career path they should take.

Normalisation. Statements about what you *ought to* do.

Nurturing parent. Stored experiences of approval and encouragement during childhood.

Parent data. Many of the understandings we take on board in our childhood. They are, at the time, accepted uncritically. Their sources is what our parents and other authority figures (teachers, etc) say to us and to others. We infer what they think from what they say.

Practice error. A term used for errors developed, or reinforced through practice.

Representation systems. Systems though which we represent external reality in our heads, by means of mentally:
- seeing (visual system)
- hearing (auditory system)
- tasting (gustatory system)
- smelling (olfactory system)
- feeling (kinaesthetic system)

Restrictive motivation. Motivation derived from awareness of what we *have* to do. An example is revising for examinations.

Stress. The mental and physical response to a situation seen as impossible.

Synthesis. Drawing together the separate elements in an analysis to form a different, meaningful whole from that from which you started.

Trances. Naturally occurring states of mind which are disengaged from reality. Daydreaming is an example. Trances can be shared. The most extreme forms are stage hypnotism, the collective trances invoked in spiritualist endeavours and the states in which some of the American evangelical church sects evoke in their congregations. At a less extreme level, when several people are watching the same film, at the cinema, or on the television, they are in a collective trance. To an even lesser degree, when somebody is telling a story at the bar of their local pub those listening are in a mild collective trance.

Further Reading

Maximising Your Memory, Marshall, P (How To Books, 1998).
Study and Learn Marshall, P (How To Books, 2nd ed., 1997).
Superior Memory, Wilding J and Valentine J (Psychology Press, 1997).
Your Memory, Baddeley, A (Prion, 1982).

Index

ACHIEVING PERSONAL WELL-BEING
How to discover and balance your physical and emotional needs

James Chalmers

We tend to shut out natural daylight, work in soulless buildings, expose ourselves to pollution, and live on a diet of junk food. This highly original book is the result of a thorough investigation into how all these factors influence our physical and emotional welfare. It shows how daylight and the environment – including our astrological signs – determine our personality and health, and how by understanding their effects we can take steps towards achieving physical and emotional well-being. The author explores the interrelation of body and mind, and reveals how only by balancing and managing their combined needs can we achieve personal well-being in all aspects of our lives. James Chalmers BSc CEng MIEE is a scientist and an artist. In this book he combines reason and imagination to offer you a remedy for the pressures of modern living.

144pp. illus. 1 85703 272 1.

BUILDING SELF-ESTEEM
How to replace self-doubt with confidence and well-being

William Stewart

People who improve their self-esteem find that their lives take on new meaning as confidence grows and well-being is enhanced. This practical, self-help book reveals how the ravages of faulty beliefs about self can be reversed, enabling the reader to develop a firm belief in his or her attributes, accomplishments and abilities. Through a series of exercises and case studies it provides strategies for building self-esteem; it will help readers set clear goals and work steadily towards them. It is also a valuable handbook for those who work in healthcare and counselling. William Stewart is a freelance counsellor, supervisor and author. His background is in nursing, psychiatric social work, and student counselling and lecturing at a London college of nursing.

152pp. illus. 1 85703 251 9.

CONTROLLING ANXIETY
How to master fears and phobias and start living with confidence

William Stewart

Many people suffer from differing degrees of anxiety. Mild anxiety is a feeling common to us all – an unavoidable part of human personality. Severe anxiety on the other hand can control our lives. The aim of this book is to provide a knowledge base for sufferers and others, and to suggest strategies that will help people manage their anxiety and regain control of their lives. It is also a valuable handbook for those who work in healthcare and counselling. William Stewart is a freelance counsellor, supervisor and author. His background is in nursing, psychiatric social work, and student counselling and lecturing at a London college of nursing. He is author of *Building Self-Esteem* and co-author of *Learning to Counsel* in this series.

144pp. illus. 1 85703 267 5.

THRIVING ON STRESS
How to manage pressures and transform your life

Jan Sutton

The pressures of modern life make us susceptible to stress. However not all stress is negative – if managed effectively we can positively thrive on it. Peak performance stress stimulates activity, enhances creativity, and motivates us to live happy and fulfilling lives. Drawing on her experience as a counsellor, stress management and assertiveness trainer, Jan Sutton not only equips you with easily mastered strategies for conquering negative stress, she also offers you a personal development programme for building self-esteem and self-confidence. The book is complete with comprehensive case studies, illustrations, and practical activities. Jan Sutton (Dip CPC) is co-author (with William Stewart) of *Learning to Counsel* in this series.

192pp. illus. 1 85703 238 1.

MAXIMISING YOUR MEMORY
How to train yourself to remember more

Peter Marshall

A powerful memory brings obvious advantages in educational, career and social terms. At school and college those certificates which provide a passport to a career depend heavily on what you can remember in the exam room. In the world of work, being able to recall details which slip the minds of colleagues will give you a competitive edge. In addition, one of the secrets of being popular with customers and friends is to remember their names and the little things which make them feel they matter to you. This book explains clearly how you can maximise your memory in order to achieve your academic, professional and personal goals. Peter Marshall is a member of the Applied Psychology Research Group of the University of London and works primarily on research into superior memory. He recently assisted with the production of Channel 4's *Amazing Memory Show*. He is also author of *How to Study and Learn* in this series.

128pp. illus. 1 85703 234 9.

MANAGING YOUR PERSONAL FINANCES
How to achieve financial security and survive the shrinking welfare state

John Claxton

Life for most people has become increasingly troubled by financial worries, both at home and at work, whilst the once dependable welfare state is shrinking. Today's financial world is a veritable jungle full of predators after your money. This book, now revised and updated, will help you to prepare a strategy towards creating your own financial independence. Find out in simple language: how to avoid debt, how to prepare for possible incapacity or redundancy, and how to finance your retirement, including care in old age. Discover how to acquire new financial skills, increase your income, reduce outgoings, and prepare to survive in a more self-reliant world. John Claxton is a Chartered Management Accountant and Chartered Secretary. He teaches personal money management in adult education.

160pp. illus. 1 85703 254 3. 2nd edition.

LEARNING TO COUNSEL
How to develop the skills to work effectively with others

Jan Sutton and William Stewart

Counselling skills are not only used by professional counsellors – they are relevant to a wide range of people as part of their work. They can also enhance all relationships. This practical book presents the principles of counselling and the fundamental skills involved. It is arranged in a logical sequence with exercises to work through and case studies to follow throughout the book. Jan Sutton (Dip CPC) is an independent counsellor, trainer, author and personal development consultant. She facilitates counselling and related topics for the University of Southampton and various adult education departments. William Stewart is a freelance counsellor, counsellor supervisor, and author whose background is nursing, psychiatric social work and four years as a student counsellor/lecturer.

160pp. illus. 1 85703 229 2.

HEALING THE HURT WITHIN
How to relieve the suffering underlying self-destructive behaviour

Jan Sutton

This powerful and profoundly moving book evolved from the author's unrelenting search for an understanding of the need to self-injure, misuse food or abuse alcohol. Written with compassion, this book reveals her findings. Teenagers and adults have courageously shared their harrowing stories of childhood sexual abuse, deprivation, rape, and other life traumas. They provide the reader with valuable insights into what helps relieve the associated emotional suffering. Their words will bring comfort to fellow sufferers, as well as encouraging them to reach out and seek help. It will also give those who have contact with sufferers, either personally or professionally, a deeper understanding of their condition. Jan Sutton (Dip CPC) is an experienced counsellor, with a special interest in self-injury, eating disorders and alcohol abuse.

144pp. illus. 1 85703 299 3.

How To Books

How To Books provide practical help on a large range of topics. They are available through all good bookshops or can be ordered direct from the distributors. Just tick the titles you want and complete the form on the following page.

___ Achieving Personal Well-being (£8.99)
___ Applying for a Job (£8.99)
___ Arranging Insurance (£9.99)
___ Backpacking Round Europe (£8.99)
___ Be a Freelance Journalist (£8.99)
___ Be a Freelance Secretary (£8.99)
___ Become a Freelance Sales Agent (£9.99)
___ Becoming a Father (£8.99)
___ Building Self-Esteem (£8.99)
___ Buy & Run a Shop (£8.99)
___ Buy & Run a Small Hotel (£8.99)
___ Buying a Personal Computer (£9.99)
___ Career Networking (£8.99)
___ Career Planning for Women (£8.99)
___ Cash from your Computer (£9.99)
___ Choosing a Nursing Home (£9.99)
___ Choosing a Package Holiday (£8.99)
___ Claim State Benefits (£9.99)
___ Collecting a Debt (£9.99)
___ Communicate at Work (£7.99)
___ Conduct Staff Appraisals (£7.99)
___ Conducting Effective Interviews (£8.99)
___ Controlling Anxiety (£8.99)
___ Coping with Self Assessment (£9.99)
___ Copyright & Law for Writers (£8.99)
___ Counsel People at Work (£7.99)
___ Creating a Twist in the Tale (£8.99)
___ Creative Writing (£9.99)
___ Critical Thinking for Students (£8.99)
___ Dealing with a Death in the Family (£9.99)
___ Dealing with Your Bank (£8.99)
___ Do Your Own Advertising (£8.99)
___ Do Your Own PR (£8.99)
___ Doing Business Abroad (£10.99)
___ Doing Business on the Internet (£12.99)
___ Doing Voluntary Work Abroad (£9.99)
___ Employ & Manage Staff (£8.99)
___ Find Temporary Work Abroad (£8.99)
___ Finding a Job in Canada (£9.99)
___ Finding a Job in Computers (£8.99)
___ Finding a Job in New Zealand (£9.99)
___ Finding a Job with a Future (£8.99)
___ Finding Work Overseas (£9.99)
___ Freelance DJ-ing (£8.99)
___ Freelance Teaching & Tutoring (£9.99)
___ Get a Job Abroad (£10.99)
___ Get a Job in Europe (£9.99)
___ Get a Job in France (£9.99)
___ Get a Job in Travel & Tourism (£8.99)
___ Get into Radio (£8.99)
___ Getting a Job in America (£10.99)
___ Getting a Job in Australia (£9.99)
___ Getting into Films & Television (£10.99)
___ Getting That Job (£8.99)
___ Getting your First Job (£8.99)

___ Going to University (£8.99)
___ Having a Baby (£8.99)
___ Healing the Hurt Within (£8.99)
___ Helping your Child to Read (£8.99)
___ How to Study & Learn (£8.99)
___ Investing in People (£9.99)
___ Investing in Stocks & Shares (£9.99)
___ Know Your Rights at Work (£8.99)
___ Learning to Counsel (£9.99)
___ Live & Work in Germany (£9.99)
___ Live & Work in Greece (£9.99)
___ Live & Work in Italy (£8.99)
___ Live & Work in Portugal (£9.99)
___ Living & Working in America (£12.99)
___ Living & Working in Australia (£12.99)
___ Living & Working in China (£9.99)
___ Living & Working in Hong Kong (£10.99)
___ Living & Work in New Zealand (£9.99)
___ Living & Working in the Netherlands (£9.99)
___ Living Away From Home (£8.99)
___ Making a Complaint (£8.99)
___ Making a Video (£9.99)
___ Making a Wedding Speech (£8.99)
___ Manage a Sales Team (£8.99)
___ Manage an Office (£8.99)
___ Manage Computers at Work (£8.99)
___ Manage People at Work (£8.99)
___ Manage Your Career (£8.99)
___ Managing Budgets & Cash Flows (£9.99)
___ Managing Credit (£8.99)
___ Managing Meetings (£8.99)
___ Managing Projects (£8.99)
___ Managing Your Personal Finances (£8.99)
___ Managing Yourself (£8.99)
___ Market Yourself (£8.99)
___ Mastering Book-Keeping (£8.99)
___ Mastering Business English (£8.99)
___ Master Public Speaking (£8.99)
___ Maximising Your Memory (£8.99)
___ Migrating to Canada (£12.99)
___ Organising Effective Training (£9.99)
___ Passing Exams Without Anxiety (£8.99)
___ Passing That Interview (£8.99)
___ Plan a Wedding (£8.99)
___ Planning Your Gap Year (£8.99)
___ Preparing a Business Plan (£8.99)
___ Publish a Book (£9.99)
___ Publish a Newsletter (£9.99)
___ Raise Funds & Sponsorship (£7.99)
___ Rent & Buy Property in France (£9.99)
___ Rent & Buy Property in Italy (£9.99)
___ Research Methods (£8.99)
___ Retire Abroad (£8.99)
___ Return to Work (£7.99)
___ Run a Voluntary Group (£8.99)

___	Self-Counselling (£8.99)	___	Using the Internet (£9.99)
___	Selling Your House (£8.99)	___	Winning Consumer Competitions (£8.99)
___	Setting up Home in Florida (£9.99)	___	Winning Presentations (£8.99)
___	Setting Up Your Own Limited Company (£9.99)	___	Work from Home (£8.99)
		___	Work in an Office (£7.99)
___	Spending a Year Abroad (£8.99)	___	Work in Retail (£8.99)
___	Start a Business from Home (£7.99)	___	Work with Dogs (£8.99)
___	Start a New Career (£6.99)	___	Working Abroad (£14.99)
___	Starting to Manage (£8.99)	___	Working as a Holiday Rep (£9.99)
___	Starting to Write (£8.99)	___	Working as an Au Pair (£8.99)
___	Start Word Processing (£8.99)	___	Working in Japan (£10.99)
___	Start Your Own Business (£8.99)	___	Working in Photography (£8.99)
___	Study Abroad (£8.99)	___	Working in Hotels & Catering (£9.99)
___	Study & Live in Britain (£7.99)	___	Working on Contract Worldwide (£9.99)
___	Studying at University (£8.99)	___	Working on Cruise Ships (£9.99)
___	Studying for a Degree (£8.99)	___	Write a Press Release (£9.99)
___	Successful Grandparenting (£8.99)	___	Write & Sell Computer Software (£9.99)
___	Successful Mail Order Marketing (£9.99)	___	Write for Television (£8.99)
___	Successful Single Parenting (£8.99)	___	Writing a CV that Works (£8.99)
___	Survive Divorce (£8.99)	___	Writing a Non Fiction Book (£9.99)
___	Surviving Redundancy (£8.99)	___	Writing a Report (£8.99)
___	Taking in Students (£8.99)	___	Writing a Textbook (£12.99)
___	Taking on Staff (£8.99)	___	Writing an Assignment (£8.99)
___	Taking Your A-Levels (£8.99)	___	Writing an Essay (£8.99)
___	Teach Abroad (£8.99)	___	Writing & Publishing Poetry (£9.99)
___	Teach Adults (£8.99)	___	Writing & Selling a Novel (£8.99)
___	Teaching Someone to Drive (£8.99)	___	Writing Business Letters (£8.99)
___	Thriving on Stress (£8.99)	___	Writing for Publication (£8.99)
___	Travel Round the World (£8.99)	___	Writing Reviews (£9.99)
___	Unlocking Your Potential (£8.99)	___	Writing Romantic Fiction (£9.99)
___	Understand Finance at Work (£8.99)	___	Writing Science Fiction (£9.99)
___	Use a Library (£7.99)	___	Writing Your Dissertation (£8.99)

To: Plymbridge Distributors Ltd, Plymbridge House, Estover Road, Plymouth PL6 7PZ. Customer Services Tel: (01752) 202301. Fax: (01752) 202331.

Please send me copies of the titles I have indicated. Please add postage & packing (UK £1, Europe including Eire, £2, World £3 airmail).

☐ I enclose cheque/PO payable to Plymbridge Distributors Ltd for £ [   ]

☐ Please charge to my ☐ MasterCard, ☐ Visa, ☐ AMEX card.

Account No. [| | | | | | | | | | | | | | |]

Card Expiry Date [|] 19 ☎ **Credit Card orders may be faxed or phoned.**

Customer Name (CAPITALS) ....

Address ....

.... Postcode ....

Telephone........................... Signature ....

Every effort will be made to despatch your copy as soon as possible but to avoid possible disappointment please allow up to 21 days for despatch time (42 days if overseas). Prices and availability are subject to change without notice. [Code BPA]